Getting Higher

The Manual of Psychedelic Ceremony

by Julian Vayne

If the doors of perception were cleansed every thing would appear to man as it is, Infinite.

– William Blake

Is everybody in?

Is everybody in?

Is everybody in?

The ceremony is about to begin...

– The Doors

Independent Book Publisher

First published by
Psychedelic Press
London, United Kingdom

Copyright © 2017
Julian Vayne and Psychedelic Press

ISBN: 9780992808877

Art: **Pete Loveday**
Design & Typesetting: **Peter Sjöstedt-H**

Originally printed in the United Kingdom

For more information:
psychedelicpress.co.uk
theblogofbaphomet.com
psychedelicmuseum.net

Naturally this book is in no way intended to promote any illegal activity and readers are encouraged to be familiar with the relevant legislation concerning psychedelic substances in their region.

Books by the same author:

Dedication

This book is dedicated to those shamans, alchemists, witches and wild wonderers who have walked these ways before us.

CONTENTS

Foreword

The way out, man, is inside

Just around the turn of the millennium—having recently radically rearranged my worldview on an extended trip to Mexico with nothing but Schultes and Hofmann's *Plants of the Gods* as my travel guidebook—I embarked on a PhD in parapsychology. Fusing these interests, I started scouring the literature for anything I could find on the overlap of drugs and magic but was shocked to find only two dedicated books were available on the subject. One was a pretty sketchy anthology of vaguely related essays and the other was a self-published yet fine, practical, and historical romp through the ups and downs of magical drug taking; *Pharmakon: Drugs and the Imagination* (2001, El Cheapo), by Julian Vayne. Fifteen years later there's still no better book on the subject.

Now, teetering on the rim of the 50th anniversary since the psychedelic peak of the 1967 Summer of Love, this book could not come at a better time. Five decades since the sixties' ultimate explosion of colour, language, fashion, music, art, therapy, intoxication, innovation, counterculture and, shortly after, 'drug' prohibition, we are now witnessing a full blown psychedelic renaissance. Some are even announcing that 2017 will be the third Summer of Love (the second being sprawled across the late eighties rave scene in the UK).

This revitalised interest in psychedelics also comes with two prongs, and both have been successful in helping these substances re-infiltrate overground culture, only this time without the media hysteria. The first is the steadily increasing amount of sober scientific research studies giving these prohibited substances to humans—unsurprisingly (re)discovering all manner of positive potential uses for them, from treating addictions, depression and anxiety to creative problem solving, helping generate new brain cells, reducing inflammation and boosting the immune system.

The second prong is less obvious in the media spotlight but has pierced the zeitgeist just as deep, and that is the steady rise in the attendance of 'medicine circles', driven largely by South American ayahuasca tourism and the mushrooming number of medicine groups operating in Europe, the US and elsewhere. It's more with this latter phenomenon of shamanic, rather than 'Western medicine' circles that this book chimes.

The current tide of overseas seekers flocking to indigenous 'shamans' in the Americas, in particular, has never been greater, and Western psychedelic neo-shamans are popping up like *Psilocybe* mushrooms on a Welsh mountainside in autumn. Indeed, given that flying to Peru to hack one's neuro wetware or slither with the plant spirits of a foreign cosmology has an ecological, economic and cultural shelf life, many are increasingly turning to the home-grown substances of their native lands and rummaging around furtively, trying to assemble some authentic and useful ritual structure for their empyrean entheogenic endeavours.

Others may have come to psychedelics through more leisurely and less exotic recreational consumption, to just get high, wig out, have a laugh and get their groove on the dance floor. But any sustained gaze into one's stash bag will ultimately give rise to some extraordinary experiences and have anyone with any wisdom reaching to go deeper and explore the ritual use of these magical molecules.

It's with gratitude to Julian then, once again, that his writing has, quite literally, leaped into the void. Because not only will this be an invaluable text for guiding those seeking their own way on a ritual psychoactive path with few signposts from Western culture—leading to safer, saner and more successful voyages—but because it does so by assuming so little about the reader's own worldview. So I'd like to celebrate the writer's rare inclusivity in accommodating even atheist animism and magic for muggles in a handbook for psychedelic ritual. Such an active agnostic perspective of encouraging the reader to just act "as if" the enchanted is actual comes no doubt from his extensive experience with chaos magic, as well as other, more traditional, occult practices.

It's this vast experience of the well-initiated that also enriches this handbook with so many ingenious and imaginative examples of rituals that can, hypothetically let's say, be performed, some of which sound delightfully familiar. Whatever transformation you seek, from disintegration to integration, you're ultimately on your own, but it never hurts to have some sage wisdom to guide you. Read on. Love long and perspire. Ahoy!

David Luke

La Gomera

November 2016

Further Forward

This manual is intended to help a wide range of people; from those with previous experience of using drugs to those who are relatively new to this territory. It is particularly for those who have encountered, or would like to encounter, the use of drugs as part of spiritual practice.

Some readers will have heard about, or perhaps taken part in, ceremonies where psychedelic substances are used. Their interest may centre on the therapeutic, spiritual or exploratory use of these drugs. Others may simply want ideas about how to enhance their chemical experiences and get really high. Often our intentions may be a combination of these desires.

While at time of writing the use of psychedelic drugs is heavily restricted, in various regions of our planet, there is an increasing recognition (alongside increasing evidence of medicinal value) that their use is a matter of personal cognitive liberty and a legitimate form of cultural identity, religious expression and spiritual practice. As our cultures struggle to make the transition, from the 'War On Drugs', (or more accurately the 'War On Some People Who Use and Supply Some Drugs'), to a more intelligent relationship with these fascinating chemicals, many individuals are searching for resources to help them. I hope this book goes some way towards meeting this need.

This is a manual of techniques for people who want to explore these drugs in a safe, sane and consensual way for spiritual illumination, personal transformation and ecstatic communion. While numerous accounts of 'spiritual' drug use are available online, and scattered through various texts (including my previous works) this volume attempts to bring together many of the ways that can be used to guide the psychedelic experience. Some of the methods presented here are ceremonial approaches, derived from both contemporary practice and traditional 'shamanic' rituals. Others are simple psychological 'hacks' designed to enhance the experiences that drugs, particularly psychedelic drugs, can provide.

This book doesn't assume any particular belief system on the part of the reader. As it draws from several modern and archaic spiritual traditions, it uses language derived from each of these contexts. For this reason, the 'drugs' in question are sometimes described here as 'sacraments', (sacred) 'medicines' or (in more modern language) 'entheogens' (substances that allow us to discover the divine within us). For the same reason the person taking the drug is sometimes described as the 'magician', 'shaman' or (in more modern language) 'practitioner' and 'psychonaut'.

The indigenous entheogenic traditions of my native land (the British Isles) are lost to me, and it is therefore the case that this book looks primarily towards the cultures of India and the Americas for much of its inspiration and guidance. My own knowledge does not extend in any depth to the cultures of China, Australia, Africa or many other places in the world where entheogenic cultures have existed and continue to thrive. I hope that others will be able to present the teachings from those peoples.

It is with a deep gratitude and respect to the indigenous communities that I present what I have learnt from their insights and techniques in this book. I hope that the wisdom of these distant lands may be thoughtfully employed to create new approaches to the use of entheogens and a reimagining of those that have been lost.

The aim of this manual is to help you get higher; how you choose to conceptualize the experiences you may encounter, whether as religious revelation, psychological self-transformation, occult exploration or beautiful ecstatic fun (or all of these at once) is up to you.

Stay high, stay free!

Julian Vayne
Devon
2017

Calling to the Spirits

*W*e have cleaned the house. There are fresh flowers and candles above a hearth fire that burns brightly. We have showered and dressed in comfortable clothing and are wearing the symbols of our shamanic path. As midnight passes we begin the ceremony.

A singing bowl rings out to the eight directions. Incense is lit on an altar upon which sit the sacred medicines; cannabis, tobacco and psilocybe mushrooms.

Also upon the altar is a strange gold and silver sculpture flanked by two candles. This icon is the creation of a group of magicians, a being called Izawa, the spirit of the psychedelic state. We offer it our own entheogenic experience, an offering of self to self. We have externalised the psychedelic experience into this icon so we can speak to it as we would another person. We explain to Izawa that these mushrooms are from Cornwall, that it is our will to reconnect with the ancient medicines of our place (the British Isles). We consume them; chewing slowly, tasting the deep, rich, magical earth that they, and we, grow from.

We use drums and rattles; we find a song to welcome the mushrooms. My partner brings some sweets from the kitchen and together we offer these to the image of Ganesh, the god of beginnings and breaker of obstacles, whose image sits, rotund, jolly, and increasingly Technicolor, on the mantelpiece. We chant his mantra and ask for blessing on our journey.

We make prayers with tobacco as the night goes on. Speaking to Izawa, to the Great Spirit, to ourselves and each other. Externalising our stories in language, bringing our attention to the blessings of this moment and being thankful.

Though we have locally gathered clay and other supplies for making art, instead we settle down and drift into trance. The pre-recorded music we have chosen is the vehicle for our journey inward. With eyes closed images arise, dreamlike visions and fractating, glowing machinery of intense meaningful beauty.

Later we make love, kissing and breathing together. Flesh itself becomes the clay of our magical art this night. The continuity of Life reaches back in time to heal long years of isolation, recognising underground wounds and holy joys, soothing and celebrating the deep past.

As dawn breaks we make ourselves a ritual breakfast of fruit and water. We tidy the hearth, sweeping away the detritus of the night, preparing the way to enter a new day. We burn sweet incense and open the curtains. We thank the spirits for the insights we have had in the night. Through times of meditative silence, of careful, intentional talk (spells or prayer), through song and dance, we have journeyed into the dawn.

We sit together and, as we did at the opening of the ritual, we take a breath together for the sky that is above us. A breath for the earth beneath us. A breath for the water that surrounds our island and a breath for the fire in our hearts; and embrace.

Our nightlong psychedelic ceremony is done.

Putting on warm clothes we sally forth to find somewhere quiet to watch the dawn. The sun is bright and the world sparkles in that wonderful, characteristic post-trip way.

Beside the river we blow tobacco smoke up towards the bright sun, the hearth fire of our world, then turn and head for home, for beer and tea (according to our individual preference), and sleep and dreaming.

The description of the ceremony above is the first of several accounts in this book. These are intended to provide ideas and inspiration for you to create your own practice in your own way.

But before we encounter the many ways that psychedelic drugs may be used as part of a spiritual process, let's take a look at the reasons why people may wish to explore these substances, and describe some important considerations and terminology...

The Medicine Path

Mind-altering drugs go with human spirituality the same way that music goes with human celebration. Sometimes the consciousness-changing substance is primarily symbolic (like the wine in the chalice at a Catholic Mass), other times the chemistry is central to the process (as with the use of ayahuasca by a South American curandero). Across times and cultures, psychoactive materials have been a ubiquitous part of the human experience. They may be used to generate peak experiences, like the revelations sought by mystics. They may be used instrumentally, to do something, such as an act of healing in shamanic or psychotherapeutic context. They may also be about communion, experiencing joy or empathy, and sharing those feelings with others (as happens in the Native American peyote circle or at a rave).

Psychedelic drugs can dramatically affect conscious awareness. Therefore, consideration of 'set' and 'setting' are crucial to the way a trip unfolds. 'Set' includes everything 'within' the (mind) set of the individual, their mood, expectations and memories of previous experiences. 'Setting' includes everything 'without', from the immediate environment of the trip, the presence or not of other people, through to the broader cultural backdrop (which, of course folds back into the 'set') of the experience.

The mental states that psychedelics give us access to can potentially prove as extreme as heaven or hell, and which state we find ourselves in is, in large part, determined by our orientation to the experience. For example, on LSD one might joyfully exclaim, "Look at all the little faces in the trees!" However, under less positive circumstances, the exact same perception of faces in the forest, the very same words uttered in different tones, might be imagined as unnerving, or utterly terrifying.

In a sense all experience can be conceptualised as chemical process (it is the complex interaction of chemistry that arises into your 'self' that is reading these words). Through the intelligent use of these sacred substances we can reveal, explore and change the self that we are, and by doing so, change our world.

Why Get Higher?

There are many, often overlapping, reasons that people seek out the psychedelic experience. Here are some that place particular emphasis on the transformative or spiritual aspect of getting high.

Self Exploration – More than two millennia have passed since Socrates claimed that 'the unexamined life is not worth living'. The restless desire to discover who and what we are, to explore, and to make meaning, is intrinsic to all humans. For some people drugs can be allies in that exploration. One may simply be curious as to what these states are like, especially when framed within the context of ritual practices.

Healing – Whether illness exists in the personal, psychological, physiological, social or even cultural body, psychedelic drugs can act as medicine. The healing power of these substances can appear spontaneously or may be encouraged by methods derived from psychoanalysis, shamanism and other approaches. Psychedelic drugs can combat alienation, depression, isolation and ennui, and may have clear effects on other forms of illness. This can occasionally include remission or cure of organic illnesses or chronic conditions, or at least an improved psychological relationship with such health problems.

Addictions and other debilitating psychological habits may be broken by the skilled use of psychedelics.

Numinous Experience – The peak experiences encountered by inspired individuals (mystics, shaman and prophets) can be accessed by the sacred use of drugs. Ecstasy, rapture and other often life-changing, frequently (though not exclusively) pleasurable, states can be encountered. These may be highly internalised experiences or may be intimately linked with the tripping environment (psychedelics used outdoors often provoke experiences of the natural world as sacred, enchanted, sublime etc.).

Other Realities – Psychedelics can allow us to enter what appear to be other realities or realms of experience. Whether we like to imagine that these experiences are of fantastical, internal and imaginal worlds, or represent some more objectively real realm (such as the 'astral' or a dimension populated by alien beings), is a matter for personal reflection and exploration.

Occult or Parapsychological – Substances that alter the mind may be used to empower acts of magic. This could mean prayers, Neo-Pagan spells, divination procedures, or any method that seeks to use the power of the imagination to interact with the past, present or future through occult (i.e. mysterious) means. Magical acts include techniques aimed at creating a particular external and concrete result; they may be 'acts of psychological neurohacking' (implanting positive affirmations in the mind) or may be believed to work through more esoteric processes. Psychonauts may want to conduct experiments with psychokinesis, extrasensory perception and other parapsychological phenomena while high.

Creative Insight – Drugs can be used not only to explore our own psyche and environment but can also lead to concrete insights into the arts and sciences, potentially giving rise to new artworks, technologies and other innovations. Psychedelic drugs can enhance problem solving, stimulate new ideas, and demolish conceptual or psychological blocks to creativity.

Preparation for Death – Drugs can be used to explore how it may feel to die. They can teach us the importance of 'giving up' to the experience, providing a broader perspective on our mortality and reducing anxiety about death.

Reset – Psychoactives can be used as initiatory tools to create a radical discontinuity in experience and allow the individual to experience a rebirth. Psychedelic experiences often leave the tripper feeling cleansed, empowered and physically and mentally well.

Recreation – There need not be a strict division between spirituality, play and enjoyment. 'Re-creation' itself can be a healing act, something that nourishes our souls. Psychedelics used recreationally help remind us of the simple joys of life, things we sometimes forget because we are so busy getting from A to Z that we forget there are 24 letters in between.

The enjoyment and fun of getting high may be an important reason for including psychedelic drugs in one's life. While some forms of religion encourage a belief that pleasure is morally wrong (that all the world is suffering, the body is sinful etc.) there are other spiritual beliefs (ancient, contemporary and emerging) that take a very different position. Within many Neo-Pagan cultures the idea that one should (while being mindful of the rights of others) 'follow one's bliss' or 'do what thou wilt' allows the delight in getting higher to be a legitimate expression of a life and world affirming attitude, and a valid spiritual practice.

Potentiation and Safety – A small dose of a substance may be potentiated by ritual or other procedures. Pragmatically this means that the user gets more 'bang for their buck'. Ritual techniques used to enhance the set and setting of the psychedelic experience can make that experience feel deeper, stronger and richer. Intelligent manipulation of set/setting can also help people feel safer, reducing the likelihood of 'bad trips' and other difficulties.

Neurological Benefits – Research on the effect of some psychedelics has begun to make use of technology to look at brain activity of people whilst high. My current, purely layperson, understanding of their results suggests that the classic psychedelic drugs work by causing less connectivity and/or activity in the region of the brain which acts as a processing hub (so, the part which decides what we pay attention to, and centralises many other inputs); simultaneously connectivity increases between areas which are normally isolated in their functions. These areas tend to deal with sensory inputs, and movement. This effect mimics some of the benefits of mediation. In practice this means that the sense of an ego identity gets 'turned down', whilst immediate physical environmental processing takes on strange new forms; eg 'seeing' uses more than just the visual cortex to process images; memories can be retrieved as pictures, and other areas get involved too, with notable effects. Do check the latest publications yourself, as the research continues apace; even if my take on the story is correct now, it may well be revised in a year or two!

Psychedelic drugs may provide periods of remission for people suffering degenerative neurological conditions (such as Alzheimer's). These effects can be observed at microdose levels (which cause imperceptible sensorial effects). Psychedelic drugs may enhance organic brain processes such as neuroplasticity (the ability of the brain cells to form new connections), and compounds found in some psychedelics have been shown to cause neurogenesis (neuron formation from neural stem cells) in vitro.

— — —

Easing the Journey

Once you have taken a psychedelic substance there may be (depending on the route of administration and the material in question) a delay between ingestion and the drug effect 'coming on'. Some of the techniques on this book can be used to provide a focus for attention while the drug starts working and will help put you into the right state of mind to get the most out of the experience. This approach also allows the drug effect to 'sneak up' on conscious awareness, rather than adopting a state of mind where we are expectantly waiting for something to happen (which may actually hamper the effects of the medicine). The activities in this book can also be used during the trip to stop you getting bored (which can be a problem with psychedelics that last for many hours).

Ritual and Spontaneity

Although words like 'ritual' and 'ceremony' are used in this book to describe various practices, these need not be the stilted, highly formalised styles of symbolic activity that readers may have encountered in religious or other contexts (such as military parades or civic ceremonies).

Terms such as ritual and ceremony are intended to indicate that the psychedelic drug is being taken in a way that we might describe as 'intelligent' or 'mindful'. By using the techniques in this book you are placing yourself in a certain relationship with the chemical experience. This relationship is one where we don't take 'the medicine' for granted.

Entheogenic ritual forms a frame around the psychedelic state. This frame may be carefully pre-planned, involving lots of ritual paraphernalia, specific roles within a larger or smaller group, a specially set up ritual space, and so on. At other times this frame may be minimal, such as a brief prayer or setting of intention before a substance is taken, and a simple act of giving thanks when the trip ends. In all cases the aim of the ritual, whether simple or complex is to enhance and 'hold' the psychedelic experience.

Whatever the format of the ceremony a blend of flexibility (speaking 'from the heart', spontaneity, humour and allowing the medicine to do its work) and formality (doing particular practices, staying focused and perhaps aiming for specific results) is most desirable.

The Psychoactive Triangle
Set, Setting and Substance

The drugs themselves are only part of the story. The wrapper around the substances; the set (the internal state of the person consuming the drug) and setting (the social context and environment in which it is taken) are what we need to be aware of if we are to use drugs for these spiritual, instrumental and collective ecstatic aims. Changes in any of these three variables (including the way that the substance is administered) can make tremendous differences to the way a drug experience unfolds.

This book focuses primarily on ways of manipulating set and setting to create certain effects, but before we look at these in more detail, let's consider the 'substance' part of the 'psychoactive triangle'.

Substance

Dosage

The amount of a substance used may be described by the following terminology:

> **Baseline:** the imagined 'normal' state of awareness before the drug is taken or after its effects have entirely worn off.

> **Placebo dose:** where the expectations of the user create a psychological and/or physiological effect, in the absence of any actual active drug.

> **Microdose:** a very low dose at which the psychoactive effect of the substance isn't noticed by conscious awareness, but nevertheless subtle changes in the bodymind can be observed (especially if microdosing is continued over a period of time).

> **Threshold dose:** a low dose at which the psychoactive effect is barely perceptible.

> **Effective dose:** the level at which the drug effect is clearly felt.

> **Low, medium (or 'common') and strong doses**

> **Dissociative dose:** the level at which memory function is impaired. Unconsciousness and collapse may occur.

> **LD50:** the point at which 50% of a given population of subjects are likely to die from toxic effects of a specific substance.

It's important to remember that 'baseline' is relative. Anything from having a very busy active day, being on a particular diet, through to genetic variations may make you more or less sensitive to psychoactives.

The effects of a given substance can be rated using various subjective scales. The most well known is the system developed by American biochemist Alexander Shulgin. In his book *PiHKAL: A Chemical Love Story* he describes the range thus:

- **MINUS, n. (-)** On the quantitative potency scale (-, ±, +, ++, +++), there were no effects observed.

- **PLUS/MINUS, n. (±)** The level of effectiveness of a drug that indicates a threshold action. If a higher dosage produces a greater response, then the plus/minus (±) was valid. If a higher dosage produces nothing, then this was a false positive.

- **PLUS ONE, n. (+)** The drug is quite certainly active. The chronology can be determined with some accuracy, but the nature of the drug's effects is not yet apparent.

- **PLUS TWO, n. (++)** Both the chronology and the nature of the action of a drug are unmistakably apparent. But you still have some choice as to whether you will accept the adventure, or rather just continue with your ordinary day's plans (if you are an experienced researcher, that is). The effects can be allowed a predominant role, or they may be repressible and made secondary to other chosen activities.

- **PLUS THREE, n. (+++)** Not only are the chronology and the nature of a drug's action quite clear, but ignoring its action is no longer an option. The subject is totally engaged in the experience, for better or worse.

◆　　　**PLUS FOUR, n.** (++++) A rare and precious transcendental
state, which has been called a "peak experience," a "religious
experience," "divine transformation," a "state of Samadhi"
and many other names in other cultures. It is not connected
to the +1, +2, and +3 of the measuring of a drug's intensity. It
is a state of bliss, a participation mystique, a connectedness
with both the interior and exterior universes, which has come
about after the ingestion of a psychedelic drug, but which is
not necessarily repeatable with a subsequent ingestion of that
same drug.

Methods of Absorption

Different methods of administration, from slower (eating, drinking),
through to faster (such as smoking, snorting, sublingual absorption or
anal administration), to the most rapid methods (intravenous injection
or introduction of a substance to cut or burnt skin) will often change the
quality as well as the duration of the experience. Drugs that are eaten
tend to come on slowly, gradually increase, peak (with one or more
peaks, depending on the substance used) and slowly fade out. Faster
methods of taking a drug can be more spectacular, with a sudden shift
between baseline and a strong peak experience. Sometimes these short
acting, fast trips can be helpful. Pragmatically they can allow people
to fit psychedelic experiences into their busy lives (smoked DMT for
example is sometimes referred to as a 'businessman's lunch' since a
trip may only take a matter of minutes). Slower methods of ingestion
allow the user time to adjust psychologically and physically to the
altered state, and it may be easier to integrate these slower experiences
into daily life.

The method of preparation and ingestion of a drug is both
colloquially and mystically part of the ritual of drug use. Rolling a
cannabis joint 'mindfully' can itself be a powerful spiritual practice as
well as a pragmatic necessity.

Some methods of absorbing psychedelics are quite elaborate, for
example building a sweat lodge or 'hotboxing' in order to absorb a
drug through the smoke filling the space.

Technological developments have allowed us find new ways of taking our medicines, such as the invention of the hypodermic needle and vaporising technologies.

Natural vs Artificial

While there are many opinions about the distinction between so-called 'naturally' occurring drugs and 'artificial' or 'man-made' materials, this book gives equal validity to all psychedelics irrespective of their origin.

Some observations about this nature/culture relationship include:

♦ Drugs derived from plants often have a long history and culture of use, which includes techniques for preparing, taking and supporting their effects.

♦ Most 'natural' drugs will still have gone through some kind of 'man-made' preparatory process. This may be as simple as cutting and drying (the flowers of cannabis) or complex (as with the use of fire, low pH water and complimentary plants to create the ayahuasca potion).

♦ The dosage of artificial drugs is often easier to calculate, due to homogeneity of the material, and for some substances their effects may be more predictable.

♦ Organically derived drugs are often a mixture of various substances, many of which may be psychoactive, while laboratory made substances can be much more refined. In practice this often means that 'natural' substances come on more slowly, may exhibit more body load (see below), and may be metabolised more easily (leaving less of a hangover).

◆ Organic drugs offer the possibility of cultivating the plant, mushroom or psychoactive animal and thereby developing a complex relationship with it. (The same may be said for alchemists and chemists who have the skills to synthesize substances in a laboratory.)

◆ Organic materials offer the possibility of rapid commodification, environmental overexploitation and cultural appropriation.

All of these nature/culture distinctions are open to debate, but the question of where the drugs we use come from is important. At the simplest level, if one knows (or believes) that the medicine comes from a trusted source, that it has been produced with minimal damage to other people and the planet; this is likely to encourage a positive mindset for the subsequent trip.

Drug Effects

There are many ways of categorising drugs, but broadly speaking psychoactive drugs can have three effects:

◆ There are drugs that stimulate (uppers) – such as amphetamines, cocaine and tobacco.

◆ There are drugs that sedate (downers) – such as opiates, alcohol and benzodiazepines.

◆ There are drugs that change the way the world appears (both our inner psychological state and our perceptions of outer reality) – such as the 'classic psychedelics', the tryptamines (e.g. LSD and DMT) and phenethylamines (such as Mescaline and MDMA). These drugs are usually described as psychedelics ('mind manifesting' substances). When used in a spiritual or self-transformative context these drugs can be entheogens (drugs that promote an awareness of the divine within).

Many substances contain a blend of these three properties; ketamine is both an anaesthetic agent and a powerful psychedelic, but is also capable of acting as a stimulant under certain conditions. Similarly, cannabis can make people talkative and giggly (up) and it can induce relaxation and sleep (down). It may also (especially if taken orally) produce powerful psychedelic and entheogenic effects (weird).

The psychoactive drugs most often used in spiritual contexts are the psychedelics; substances where the primary effect is to change the way we perceive things. These drugs make the world (inner and outer) look different or 'weird'. Effective psychedelics are those that have a high probability of inducing experiences of changed awareness, self-discovery, self-transformation and ecstatic, numinous states without debilitating body load or impairment of memory.

Body Load

A psychedelic drug, to be of any practical use, must be able to change awareness without causing significant physical distress or damage. While popular psychedelics work at dosages that are very safe for the whole body, they may still produce various physiological effects. As the user experiences these changes, this may in turn create a range of psychosomatic symptoms.

Psychedelic drugs often produce effects that, for most people are quite benign like yawning, dilation of the pupils or conscious awareness of normally unconscious bodily processes (such as the saccading of the eyes or the beating of the heart). However some experiences may include symptoms that the user is less comfortable with such as nausea, trembling, changes in sensitivity to temperature and other effects. Any unpleasant effects are described as the 'body load'.

An intelligent understanding of substance, set & setting can help reduce body load, often by simply giving the psychonaut something else (other than their discomfort) to focus their attention on. The mild nausea that sometimes accompanies the early stages of entheogenic explorations can be the result of both the activation of serotonin receptors in the gut, as well as the burst of adrenaline released as the body begins to register a powerful internal change. Many of the techniques contained in this book can be used to support the psychedelic explorer, thereby reducing unwanted symptoms of physical and psychological distress.

Some traditions (notably those who use organically derived drugs such as peyote and ayahuasca) actively engage with attendant phenomena such as nausea and possible vomiting, frequently conceptualizing these effects as being part of a healing, purification process.

Know Your Substance

Getting to know a particular substance, and the best ways to get high using it, takes time. Getting a taste for a drug, getting acquainted with how it works for you, learning about the pharmacology, the risks, the options for administration and, where possible developing a relationship with the plant or 'spirit' (however that is imagined) of the medicine can be a lifelong journey.

Care, sensitivity and intelligence should be used, especially when beginning work with a novel (e.g. newly discovered or never-before-consumed by the individual) substance. It is a really good idea to seek out reliable online and printed sources before taking any drug, especially a newly synthesized one where effects are still unclear. It is wise to take a threshold or low dose to begin with, to establish that the consumer does not have an idiosyncratic reaction or allergic response. The dose-response curve (the way the effects of a drug increases at different dosage levels) should be understood. For some materials, such as 2C-B or the NBOM-e series, the dose-response curve is very steep. This means that, for example, taking twice a 'standard' dose may actually be many times stronger than a single dose (rather than just twice as strong). Some recently synthesized psychedelics (marketed as 'research chemicals') can have dangerous, even life-threatening effects at doses not far above the 'standard' amount.

Naturally not everyone reacts the same way to a given substance, and some substances may sit more or less easily with a particular person. Careful exploration and reflection are the keys to getting to know which substances are your allies, which ones work in different circumstances, and which ones it makes sense to avoid.

When combining drugs it is important not to make the (potentially fatal) mistake of mixing substances that do not sit happily together. That said advanced practitioners might wish to carefully explore relationships between substances that may superficially seem chemically contra-indicated or experientially very different. From such adventures have come insights such as the way that peyote (which contains phenylethylamines) and ayahuasca (which contains mono-oxidase inhibitors such as harmaline) can in fact be combined without any undue problems (theoretically this combination could lead to a hypertensive crisis, i.e. out of control blood pressure; which can occur if pharmaceutical mono-oxidase inhibiting drugs and phenylethylamines such as MDMA are combined). Blending drugs may be informed by the relationship of the states of awareness they generate. For example ketamine, which changes the sense of the body in space, can be spectacularly combined with 2C-B (a highly somatic phenylethylamine which can enhance touch, smell and taste). This push-me-pull-you combination can help the user consciously recall the extreme depersonalised states induced by ketamine. This combination may also make possible sensual, erotic and other types of bodywork that would be unlikely to succeed with ketamine alone.

Some drugs exhibit cross-tolerance with other substances as well as other effects with repeated administration. Within a single session an initial dose of a medicine, followed by additional ('booster') doses, may be used. For some substances, used in particular contexts (such as the psychotherapeutic use of MDMA) protocols for dosing have been developed by researchers. For other substances, used in other environments, it may be a case of relying on inspiration, informed intelligence and intuition to know how much to take of what and when.

The Bow Wave

Just as a ship travelling through water has a bow wave that precedes it, it is possible for a psychedelic trip to begin very soon after a drug has been taken, sometimes faster than should be theoretically possible. This effect, which can occasionally begin even before the drug is consumed, is driven by anticipation, excitement and anxiety (and perhaps some mysterious occult effect). Such a 'bow wave' encounter may indicate that the experience will be a powerful and deeply transformative one.

Paradoxically, it can also be the case that a drug may take far longer to come on than is suggested in the literature (or on the basis of previous experience). This may be due to what the psychonaut has eaten or to a range of other psychological and physiological factors (remember; 'baseline' is a relative term). It is worthwhile remembering that one of the most common experiences with psychedelics is thinking that the drug hasn't worked; taking more, then realising that the effects are beginning and now you've taken more than your intended dose...

Contact High

It is possible that members of a group, who may not have taken a substance, can experience changes in awareness simply by being in the presence of others who are tripping. This phenomenon is known as 'contact high' and is perhaps caused by the fact that the self we are, as well as being a 'product' of our own bodymind, is also something that emerges through our relationships with others (and is in turn affected by their state of mind). This phenomenon may allow people who don't want to use a particular substance to participate in a psychedelic session and still get high.

Beginning the Journey

Psychedelic drugs radically rearrange our experience of the world. They cleanse the doors of perception, so that the most mundane of things can be appreciated as wonderful, curious and even divine. In seeing the world as though for the first time we have the opportunity to be deeply aware of it. Everyday actions such as breathing, walking, eating or dancing may become opportunities for simultaneously mindful and spontaneous action, provoking experiences that are pregnant with meaning and sacred, magical possibility.

Within many cultures, the use of psychedelics is often collective and participatory. In contrast, psychedelic sessions in a (licensed) modern medical context usually involve a subject and guide (or therapist). In the latter scenario it is often only the subject who takes the drug. The sitter or therapist is present to help the voyager on their journey, guiding them to address issues (such as traumatic memories) to gain personal insight and healing. (The therapist will have taken the drug themselves in a therapeutic setting during their training.)

In 'traditional' contexts, even if a shaman is acting in a therapeutic role similar to that of the psychotherapist, the shaman also takes the medicine (indeed the shaman is often the person who takes the largest dose of the drug while still managing to successfully run the ceremony).

Setting Out

Whether we are taking drugs in a guided context, as part of a shamanic ritual with others or alone we can be mindful of preparing the space (the Setting) and ourselves (the Set) to optimise the experience. Here are a few things you might consider doing before tripping

Washing the body is a common act of preparation. This could mean using a bath or shower, or simply washing one's hands. Brushing hair, adding or removing make-up, selecting how we are dressed, putting on special jewellery; all these things can be considered as investments in the self; nourishing and attentive acts that help us enter the drug experience with a good set.

Fasting or other dietary changes can potentiate drugs that are eaten, making them more easily absorbed. Fasting can help psychologically prepare the psychonaut (by building anticipation) and reduce body load (especially nausea). Depending on which sacrament is being used, some types of food should be avoided (for example fermented foods if the drug contains a mono-oxidase inhibitor); good research is important in this respect.

The psychonaut may choose to wear suitable loose fitting clothes so that movement is unrestricted. The look and feel of clothing can be more significant in a charged environment, to yourself and those with you, so choose with care. Blankets are useful items for both indoor ceremonies and outdoor adventures, providing practical warmth, something to sit on, shade from the sun, and a comforting sense of security.

In preparing the space, especially if the psychedelic journey will take place wholly or predominantly in one location, it is important to create a supportive, ideally beautiful, setting. This may entail elaborate decoration, or some simple act such as mindfully taking the rubbish out of the house and sweeping the floor.

Actively helping to shape the environment (whether by lighting candles or investing time installing fabulous artworks for a rave) is a powerful way to ensure a good set as well as setting.

The presence of patterned fabrics (such as Indian paisley designs or Shipibo textiles), stone walls, wooden floors etc. can provide interesting surfaces that, during the psychedelic experience, may morph, ripple and transform in a multitude of ways. With this in mind some psychedelic traditions prefer to use plain black or white clothing and neutral hangings, in order to reduce external stimulation and direct the focus of the experience elsewhere.

The presence of artworks, images of deities, flowers, incense and other objects, both natural and human-made, can help create a space conducive to a profound, joyous, and transformative experience. These objects need not be of a 'hippie ethnic' style. If one finds it empowering to have a poster of a pop star or picture of a sports car in the environment, then these objects should be used.

Ensure that practical considerations are addressed, turn off the phone, make water for drinking available. Prepare any other paraphernalia in advance of the trip. Try to ensure that you have comfortable seating, cushions and a suitable level of ventilation and warmth in the space.

While some experiments may be conducted in darkness, light is often an important consideration, whether from artificial or natural sources. Candles, lamps and electrical lights all have their uses, with the presence of real flames being something that many practitioners favour.

The use of lighting is a simple way of inducing and directing trance states. As sighted people absorb the vast majority of their information about the universe through their eyes, strobes, dream-machines, flickering candles, computer visualizers and other methods can be easily employed to explore and direct the psychedelic experience. A joss stick placed so that a candle flame illuminates its smoke can be an enchanting sight on psychedelics and may provide an engaging focus of attention for quite some time.

Moving a visual stimulus through a sequence could itself be used to create a ceremonial journey. This could be a series of different strobe rates designed to have specific neurological effects, or a sequence of coloured lights accorded some symbolic meaning (for example the colours connected with the chakras in Eastern esoteric anatomy, or those associated with the spheres of the Hermetic Qabalah).

If the experience is an indoor night time journey, the timing of when the curtains are opened in the morning can provide a dramatic step change of mood. Choose your moment wisely!

The Culture of Trust

Entheogenic experiments, whatever the details of their intention and structure, should happen within a culture of mutual trust and respect. For group work this means being clear with participants about the material and doses being used, ensuring that people respect the rules and culture of the group.

Personal disclosures expressed during the psychedelic process should be handled sensitively. Group members are encouraged to be open, honest, to stay with the process until its end, and not to confuse their own personal drama or revelations with something that necessarily needs to be shared with, or will be relevant to, other people. (If God has just told you in a drug-induced vision that you are the Messiah it may be wise to wait a while after the experience, in order to reality test and integrate this in your day-to-day life, rather than announcing this 'fact' to all and sundry during or immediately after the session.)

Prayers, Spell and Invocations

In many cultures when we drink alcohol, we make a toast. We cast an enchantment or prayer into the moment of ingesting that mind-altering substance, wishing ourselves good health, bravery, happiness and other blessings.

Before taking a psychedelic drug some psychonauts like to say a prayer or set an intention. It can be helpful to address the substance as an intelligent spirit entity and to talk to it. It matters very little if this attitude is seen as a pragmatic psychological trick or because the sacred plants you're planning to consume are actually the expressions of independent, cognisant entities (ancestors, spirits, gods or whatever). Human neurology has developed to interface with other conscious minds (located in other people) and sometimes the strategy of addressing apparently inanimate objects (be they sacred drugs, boats, cars or photocopiers) as beings with their own personalities can work wonders. This strategy sets up a personal, emotional and intimate connection with the substance being used. The prayer may be as simple as 'Spirits of LSD, protect and inspire us!'

Shamanic practitioners may call (aloud or silently) on their guides and spirits during ceremony, petitioning mythical figures connected with the medicines they are using. If you wish, you could research the substance you are using to learn about its mythology. Newer molecules may not have an established symbolic vocabulary but new associations can be discovered by getting to know the novel substance and 'listening' to what the 'spirit' of the drug (in your experience) 'likes'.

Within the entheogenic experience itself a belief in parapsychological, panpsychic or animist views of the universe can also be tremendously useful. Afterwards we may enjoy exploring other interpretations of what's going on, and even smile at our belief in such 'impossible' things. Some practitioners may think of these approaches as pragmatic 'psychology hacks' or methods of 'sleight of mind'. However we prefer to understand these processes, maintaining a playful, open-minded and curious attitude to what we experience would seem to be the best policy.

If the medicine is to be used for a specific process such as healing or transformation, then a statement of intent (SOI) may be made at the beginning of the ceremony. Within the modern Western magical tradition, part of the discipline of creating a SOI is that it forces the practitioner to think through their intention very clearly and to find a wise and clear way to express this in language. An SOI may be expressed in a clever linguistic way (for example to suggest that the desired event has already happened) or simply as a clear statement of desire; 'It is our will that...'

People from post-Christian (and especially post-Protestant) or atheist cultures may feel some uncertainty about the idea of prayers or spells and more generally about how they should conduct themselves in a ceremonial setting. What matters is intention, not complex or theatrical phrasing. What matters is authenticity.

In a ritual context it is usual to keep chitchat to a minimum, so when we speak we do so with intention and awareness but also spontaneity and 'for real'. Experience of the ritual 'flow state' comes with practice, so don't be afraid. Know you are in a safe space, whether alone or with others, and speak your truth.

Opening Rituals

In many spiritual traditions, ritual actions are used to psychically prepare the space in which a ceremony is about to take place.

Some traditions focus on the idea of opening or casting a circle, or of orientating the self in relation to various metaphysical concepts, but whatever terms are used the practice is essentially the same: Know where you are.

Once the ritual space is ready (physically clean, paraphernalia prepared, the location secured and telephones turned off) the symbolic perimeter of a psychological safe space is described. Obstructions and problems are imagined as being sent away and 'good vibes' (spirits, attitudes etc.) are invited in.

Here is an example of an opening ritual:

Opening the Doors of Perception

Having completed all other preparations of the environment the psychonaut(s) stand in the space where they plan to take the substance. They may be staying in this room for the duration of the trip or using it only as the 'launch pad' environment and will later head out to walk in nature, go to a party, explore the rest of the building etc.

There is a moment of silence.

One person rings a singing bowl or bell and says:

'Attention, attention, attention! We are present in the Now, in this place. We let go any confusion and tension and are fully here in this wonderful moment.'

Participants(s) then stand and face the east (or some other symbolic direction to be decided by the style of the group and/or the architecture of the space).

One person says, "May the doors of perception be cleansed". At this the participants move their hands as though opening a door, or drawing back a curtain. The aim here is to imagine this 'cleansing' happening in the space through the power of this symbolic action. (Practitioners may like to visualisation a brilliant psychedelic light entering the space from the direction in question.)

This process is repeated while facing each of the remaining cardinal points.

Participants then reach down and touch the earth and words are spoken; 'May we be supported and nourished by the earth'.

Then reaching up to the sky, 'May we be inspired and high as the stars above us!'

Participants enjoy another moment of silence before proceeding to take the sacrament.

Depending on the style of the group, the space being used and other considerations, these rituals may be more or less elaborate. A common approach in many traditions is to 'call in' the spirits of the four directions, represented by the elemental qualities associated with air, fire, water and earth (and perhaps other directions; above, below and the centre). Symbolic colours or animals may be taken as emblems of these qualities (e.g. a hawk for air in the east, a fish for water in the west etc.) depending on the tradition in question. These symbols may be physically depicted (using banners or other icons in the space), called in with spoken invocations at each direction, and/or visualised by the participants.

For some ceremonies psychonauts may wish to emphasize the protective aspect of these practices (for example, demarking the boundary of the space with salt and water to symbolically purify it) or drawing (in the air, again with suitable visualisation) a circular perimeter, or other symbols. This kind of activity is intended to ward off malevolent or disruptive forces, to empower the participants and charge the space with magical power.

At the end of a psychedelic ceremony it is usual to use a practice to formally end the session. This may be as simple as giving silent thanks to the spirits of the medicine, the spirits of the place and the time, or may have a more complex form. Here's an example of a closing practice.

Closing Ceremony

Participants hold hands for a moment and breathe together. One person says:

"We return to baseline, inspired and informed by the sacrament we have taken together. May we each manifest in our lives the wisdom we have found for the benefit of ourselves and all beings."

A bell is sounded.

Participants face the first direction:

"We thank the sacrament for opening the doors of perception'.

At these words a gesture is made as though closing a door or drawing a curtain.

This process is repeated at each direction.

Then touching the earth "We thank the earth for supporting and nourishing us".

Then reaching up, "we thank the stars for guiding us".

Participants hold hands again (or stand in the centre if the ritual is a solo affair).

One person says, "we thank all the spirits for this excellent adventure'.

Using these techniques we create a setting for psychedelic drugs that optimises their effects and enhances their entheogenic potential.

Core Techniques

Here are some of the essential tools to help you navigate the psychedelic experience. You may want to try out some of these practices before you get high. As part of daily life, bodywork practice (such as yoga or tai chi) and meditative practice (such as mindfulness meditation) help tone the physical and psychic muscles, creating optimum conditions for the psychedelic experience.

Breathwork

Breathing provides a vital connection between our bodies and our awareness. Controlling breathing is one of the simplest techniques for changing our awareness, with or without the use of drugs.

As we become more stimulated or agitated, the speed of respiration increases and the volume of air exchanged tends to decrease. During difficult or intense parts of the trip, deliberately slowing and deepening the breath serves to calm the bodymind as a whole.

The breath is a wonderful focus for the mind when tripping. When high we can reflect on the fact that our first act when we are born is to breathe in, and our last before we die is to breathe out. Breath happens unconsciously but can be controlled with conscious effort. Awareness of the breath (such as during mediation) allows us to notice this process but not change it. We can hold our breath and then release our psychic tensions along with the air as we exhale. We can share the rhythm of breathing with other people and enter a group communion that is deeper than words.

Here are some examples of breath techniques to try:

Hawk Breath

Stand with your feet about shoulder width apart. Raise the arms up and out to the sides making a motion as though lifting up imaginary wings while breathing in. Bring the hands together with arms outstretched above your head. Now breathe out, perhaps forcefully through the mouth, as you lower your hands straight down the front of the body. Touch either your heart or tan tien (just below the navel, the body's literal centre of gravity and the root from which we grow in the womb). Repeat this process; again sweeping the arms out and up, then down, touching the body.

There are many variations of this technique including bringing the hands together in front of an object (the sun, the moon, or a candle flame for instance). As the hands meet they form a circle or triangle, framing the focus of the gaze. As the practitioner breathes they imagine they are absorbing 'energy' from the selected focal point into their bodymind.

Sun Moon Breath

The index finger of one hand is placed between the eyes (over the ajna or 'third eye' chakra in Hindu esoteric anatomy). The thumb reaches down so that it can close either the left or right nostril. Many variations of the technique exist. One approach is to begin with some full, deep breaths through both nostrils. The thumb is then used to close the right nostril. Breath is drawn in through the left nostril and as this happens the practitioner imagines that they are drawing in 'ida' the lunar force, the yin energy of the universe. This energy is often visualised as light, glowing the colour of the full moon. The lunar breath is imagined suffusing the body, opening the bodymind up to the power of the receptive yin quality in the universe. The breath then exits the same left nostril, the right nostril remains closed and the process is repeated several times. The thumb is then used to close the left nostril and bright, solar, 'pingala' or yang energy is drawn in through the right. Again this energy is felt as radiating through the body, often visualised as sunlight.

Once these lunar and solar breaths have been drawn into the body, at a point when the practitioner perceives some effect, the cycle ends and breath is drawn in through both nostrils. Some yogis will contract the perineum muscle at this point with the intention of rousing Kundalini, the psychosexual earth energy symbolised as a coiled fire snake at the base of the spine.

This practice can be considered a healing ritual in that it aims to create a balance in these three elements (ida, pingala and kundalini) in the Hindu esoteric anatomy. It can also be used to induce various ecstatic states and revelatory experiences.

Partner and Group Breathing

In small groups of two or more people it is possible to experiment with passing a breath around the circle or between companions. Facing each other, as one person breathes out the other breathes in and so on. This practice can be very intimate and bonding for the participants and may be used to create entrained (synchronized) brainwaves and trance states.

Breathwork Systems

Approaches such as Holotropic Breathwork (developed by Stanislav Grof) or Rebirthing-breathwork (by Leonard Or) and other methods have been developed in recent years. Many of these breathwork methods use controlled versions of hyperventilation, and are capable of causing significant changes in awareness with or without drugs (especially if performed over a long period of one of more hours). These techniques can be usefully combined with psychoactive substances by experienced practitioners.

Light Breath and Tonglen

A popular breath technique, sometimes called Light Breathing, is simply breathing in positive energy (this is imagined, for instance as white light) and breathing out any constricting or negative forces (perhaps visualised as black smoke). A practice like this may be continued until the breath out is as radiant and clear as the inhalation.

The Tibetan Tonglen meditation works in a similar manner to the Light Breath (but in reverse), by breathing in negative energy and, after alchemically transforming this by the presence of one's 'good heart', breathing out positive, compassionate blessing and good thoughts towards others (the word Tonglen literally means 'giving and receiving'). This practice can be used to develop empathy and to wish others the strength to overcome adversity. Tonglen can also be used to overcome enemies; by breathing in their negative attitude and breathing out your own positive regard for them (thus taking away much of their attempted psychic power over you as an intended victim). The focus of the purifying breath may be a person, group, or even an aspect of the self (such as a memory or addiction).

In Tonglen first we breathe in our own suffering, and then breathe out positive regard and compassion for ourselves. The breath and intention is then imagined as extending to other people whom we love (the practitioner breathes in the suffering from friends, internally transmutes it, and breathes out compassion). The intention/breath is then directed towards people we know but are not close to, then to people with whom we have difficult relationships, and finally to all sentient beings. In this practice the practitioner uses the transformative power of their own compassionate Buddha nature (i.e. capacity to recognize the difficulties we all face) to transform suffering into liberation and peace.

Meditation

It is sometimes said that drugs don't go well with meditation, but that meditation goes wonderfully with drugs. While there are numerous approaches to meditation, 'mindfulness' (of breath) is one of the simplest and in some respect is very likely to be part of a psychonaut's practice.

Mindfulness meditation is used as a tactic to allow us to experience things as they are now. It has well attested therapeutic and adaptive benefits including reduced anxiety, increased emotional and cognitive capacity, reduction of pain (both psychological and physical) and so forth. Without being in any kind of extraordinary state of consciousness, mindfulness meditation allows us to explore our current 'baseline' reality; it is a valuable complement to psychedelic practice.

The usual technique of mindfulness meditation is to sit in a comfortable, alert and relaxed posture (e.g. lotus, half-lotus, cross-legged or on a straight backed chair or stool). Attention is brought to the breath and the meditator becomes aware of the sensation of breathing without attempting to affect it in any way (although it will tend to slow and deepen). Within very little time other thoughts will arise into awareness and the meditator will find they are thinking about the past, planning the future or focusing on other inner or outer sensations (a rumbling stomach or the sound of a ticking clock). Noticing the appearance of these thoughts, the meditator brings their awareness back to the breath. Sometimes practitioners like to label their thoughts once they notice them; 'thinking about what I'm going to do after this meditation session', and then return their attention to the breath.

Coming back to an awareness of the breath is done gently and with great compassion for the Self. Drifting away from being attentive is a natural mental process and should be expected. Attention is brought back to the breath with an understanding of the fact that this process is, in itself, mindfulness meditation: Paying attention to the breath, drifting off on a train of thought, noticing this is happening and returning concentration to the breath (before the cycle repeats...) is the practice. The aim is emphatically not to empty the mind of all sensations or to hold awareness rigidly in one place (there are plenty of trance techniques and other mediation styles that call for that).

Mindfulness meditation can be beneficial before and after (and sometimes during) entheogenic experiences. It may be useful as a centring tool if the practitioner is finding the intensity of the trip difficult to embrace. As with many of the approaches described here, prior practice and familiarity with the technique enhances the ability (and enjoyment!) of using it whilst high.

Various states of awareness can emerge during mindfulness sessions (even without drugs) including physical sensations (heat, cold or tingling in the limbs for example), brilliant ideas and even religious visions. In all cases the aim, during the session, is to be conscious of what is going on and (unless of course it is a stimulus that should be acted on—such as a fire alarm) to notice the thought, smile inwardly (for these shifts in concentration are in the nature of mind), and return to awareness of the breath.

A period of mindfulness meditation can be beneficial before tripping. If particular thoughts repeatedly arise when the attention wanders from the breath these can be a useful guide to the practitioner's mind set. This can help the practitioner identify an issue or formulate a question which they hope to explore in the psychedelic state. It can also act as a warning that the mind may be too full of anxiety or obsessive thoughts for the psychedelic experience to be an easy journey. The psychonaut may wish to wait until their set is different, or put additional measures in place to support their psychedelic experience (such as asking for the help of a guide).

Other forms of meditative practice can also be combined with psychedelics. Practices such as object concentration (for example contemplating a mandala, a mirror, a flower or something else), the use of mantras and other meditative methods can be very interesting during drug-enhanced states.

Sound

Music is the most universal and powerful way of affecting the psychedelic experience. Appreciation of music is greatly enhanced by the vast majority of psychedelic drugs.

Pre-recorded Music

Careful selection and use of pre-recorded music is part of the skill of the modern shaman (and DJ). It is important to consider the progression (rise, peak and fall) of pre-recorded music in terms of the progression of your ceremony and the substance(s) being used. Forethought into which tracks to have available, and their easy accessibility, is vital to the smooth flow of sounds; altered states of awareness sometimes make usually simple tasks (like getting your laptop to play music) seem rather tricky! It can also be useful to check out noise levels whilst sober, so that the volume does not become a point of concern during the trip.

Listening to music provides both a wrapper around the trip and interesting content to focus on while high. A whole psychedelic journey can be shaped and directed by the appropriate use of pre-recorded music. For inward journeys headphones, low light levels and a great sound track may be all you need whereas for shared journeys, at a festival or concert, it is the music that binds people together.

Ambient music may be useful during some psychedelic experiments. The sound of singing bowls, rushing water, the rainforest or white noise can help mask distracting sounds (such as the sound of your neighbours watching TV) as well as helping to give the psychedelicized mind some content to focus on. Complex layered sound can be particularly interesting at the peak of a trip. This could be of the intense trance-dance techno variety, or the rising and falling of tone generator waveforms in compositions in the 'drone' genre.

'Human scale' music (featuring acoustic instruments, vocals and gentle rhythmic beats) with an uplifting quality is often favoured as listening material towards the end of a trip. Dub, reggae and folk compositions can help return us to the everyday world from the far-out spaces of the psychedelic state.

Making Music

While listening to music can be great when you're tripping, making it can sometimes be even better. In many shamanic and Neo-Pagan contexts the use of chants, call and response songs and other sounds remind us of the fact that collective music making is an essential part of human culture. We make music in situations where group bonding (e.g. sporting events or military ceremonies) is desired and/ or altered states of awareness are present (e.g. religious settings). Whether tripping alone or with others, singing and making music allows the psychonaut to find a form of expression that can feel deeper than language. Making music can thus both frame the psychedelic experience and also act as an expression of it.

The use of music is perhaps one of the defining features of shamanic practice. The shaman may lead the ritual (or parts of it) by making music and singing while others listen or the creation of a soundscape may be a fully communal activity.

Even if you are not a skilled musician try experimenting with various musical instruments while high. These could be anything from electronic devices through to rattles or mouth harps. Instruments tuned using the pentatonic scale (so notes played can't sound off key) may be useful for non-musicians to play with.

Experiments with discordant sound (or forms of 'white noise') can be rewarding as psychedelics can assist us to discern harmonies, or even what could be words, in an apparently chaotic cacophony.

Musicians may find that they are still able to play successfully while high on psychedelics. They may even be objectively more skilful and are certainly likely to become swept up more easily into their own music.

Drumming

The quintessential shamanic tool is the drum. (Whereas typical Western depictions of magicians often include a wand or staff, those of shamans often include a drum. In this sense a shaman corresponds to a wizard, employing their wand as a beater and the drum as their pentacle of the magical art.)

Percussive rhythms have demonstrable effects on various neurological processes and can be used to induce a variety of altered states of awareness with or without the use of drugs. The drum is a metaphorical horse; the rhythm of the steed that the psychonaut 'rides' through the trip. It provides a convenient and continuous presence that we can focus our attention on, echoing the rhythmic pulse of our hearts and the other regular patterns in our bodies (and our planet), driving the ceremony forward.

When using drum(s) in a formalised group ceremonial setting it can sometimes be helpful to have a particular rhythm to work with. In the Native American peyote ritual this is a simple, fast rhythm of around 200 beats per minute. In some ayahuasca ceremonies a slower, lilting rhythm is often used, with the accent on the fourth beat. The faster peyote drumming suits phenethylamine substances (with their rushing amphetamine quality), whereas the tryptamines (such as psilocybin) may blend well with slower, more complex textured rhythms.

Different substances and periods during a trip may respond differently to different rhythms; experience and experiment are the best guides. It may be useful to have regular, driving rhythms when coming up into the psychedelic state, more spacious, gentle or textured music at the peak and then joyous celebratory tunes as the descent occurs, ending with calming meditative sounds.

Suggestions for Ritual Singing Practice

Singing is a good way of directing attention (or 'energy') at a particular thing, be it a ritual object (for example one might sing over drugs, water or food before they are ceremonially consumed) or even a person in the hope of effecting healing or some other transformation. Combining qualities of creativeness, breath control, presence in the moment, communal connection, and enjoyment, singing gives us an instant and easy activity that needs no equipment other than our own bodies.

Group singing may create an immaterial 'third voice' from the harmonic resonances that arise between physical voices, a phenomenon which is particularly satisfying when enjoying extraordinary consciousness.

During a ceremony a song may 'come through', sometimes a whole composition (and for musicians it may include instrumental music as well as the tune and words). A song may also arrive into awareness as a simple collection of sounds or a single phrase that grows as it is sung. Many traditions consider that songs which emerge in the psychedelic ritual space are gifts from the spirit of the medicine.

In some rituals, especially where a particular intent is specified, a song or chant may be prepared in advance and then sung as part of the ceremony. In the altered state a predetermined song may morph and change, perhaps acquiring new words or elements during its performance.

Terence McKenna once observed that the song 'Row, row, row your boat' was a perfect modern Western icaro (a song sung during an ayahuasca session). Such deeply embedded childhood tunes, nursery rhymes, hymns and poems can be useful as means of holding our attention when tripping while allowing the transformational power of the psychedelics to do their work.

Mantras, rune names, magical words and chanting may all be employed in psychedelic ritual. Simple syllables, such as 'Om' and 'Ah' may be used, and free-form sound improvisation (such as the humming, whistling, throat singing and other sounds used by shamans) can prove effective either alone or in a group setting.

Feel free to play with sound, listen to some examples of religious, shamanic or tribal singing if you need inspiration. Instead of regarding this as performance and becoming self-consciousness, let the sound well up as an expression of the psychedelic state. Even if you are alone try singing, chanting, humming, whistling etc.

Creating a soundscape of notes, humming, guttural growls, and other vocalisations can provide a perfect backdrop to psychedelic adventures. Singing can provide an excellent focus for attention as the medicine begins to work, while even in very deep (or high) states of consciousness, vocalising is usually possible. Words may be elusive but singing can help give the psychonaut a sense of agency and feedback which acts to support them as they navigate their trip.

Movement

Synchronized dances have the effect of bringing a group together and supporting entrainment of brain patterns and cognitive processes. Freeform spontaneous dance, whether at a rave or part of a ceremonial ritual, provides an opportunity to respond at a bodily level to the sacred substances that have been ingested. Try approaches to dance where you start by stomping the feet, or moving the hands and allow the movement to develop through the whole body. More structured styles of dance work, such as the Five Rhythms approach developed by Gabrielle Roth, may be useful to engage the bodymind of the psychedelicized dancer in a particular process. (In Five Rhythms appropriate music is used to explore five styles of movement; Flowing, Staccato, Chaos, Lyrical and Stillness.)

Shaking movements, such as those used in some ecstatic Christian cultures (notably the Pentecostal denominations) can be explored. Some substances, such as psilocybin containing mushrooms, can induce energy rushes, with quivering, shivering pulses in the body, and these sensations can be worked with (and made more pleasant) by deliberately incorporating them into shaking styles of movement.

Shaking dance can be used to unblock energy channels, to ride the adrenaline shivers as a trip is coming on, to unlock what psychoanalyst Wilhelm Reich called muscle or 'body armour' (the physical tensions in our bodies that echo our psychic tensions), to promote healing and ecstatic insight.

Complex movements, such as the stomping dance of the Wixáritari (Huichol) people (three stamps left leg, then three stamps right leg, and repeat) provides the conscious mind something to focus on while the sacred medicine does its work. The elaborate Gurdjieff Movements or simpler challenges (such as rubbing your belly while patting the head) can create very interesting states of awareness when combined with psychoactives at a suitable dose. Somewhat counter-intuitive or highly symmetrical movements may also be of interest to psychonauts who wish to explore how the left and right hemispheres of the brain interact in the psychedelic state.

Some individuals find that they are able to learn complex movements very rapidly when they are high (including skills such as poi or juggling). Others (especially if the dosage of the psychedelic is rather larger) may find that psychedelic effects make learning any sequence of dance steps or other movements near impossible. Go with what moves you.

During the psychedelic trip it is useful to have a repertoire of movement practices to draw upon. These can be deployed while dancing at a rave, during a pause while walking in the landscape or within a ceremonial chamber. Explore free-form movements, simple activities (such as rolling the head and the stretches that feel right for your body) through to more elaborate approaches (such as long form Tai Chi drills).

Posture

An often overlooked aspect of embodiment that the way we hold ourselves influences our mood. When we are bored we slouch, when we are fearful we might curl up into a ball. When we are happy our bodies relax into open postures, when we are strong we stand tall and proud. It is also possible to make the arrow of somatic causality point the other way; so if one is fearful during a psychedelic adventure, try standing tall. If you are tense, try unfolding the arms and legs and consciously adopt a posture that you associate with relaxation and confidence. The feedback mechanisms of the face can be used too. Smile, even laugh if you're worried or sad. As you adopt the posture and expression of the mindset you wish to gain so the subtle psychological and somatic feedback begins to operate. In short, fake it 'til you make it.

The mirror neurons in our brains mean that the postures and expressions that we observe in others also directly affect our own state of mind. This is an important factor for group psychedelic sessions and should be considered when we are tripping with other psychonauts, especially those who may be having challenging experiences.

Balance

Psychonauts may like to explore balancing skills while high. This may be the use of balance yoga postures, such as Garudasana (eagle pose), Vrikshasana (tree pose), balancing techniques from other styles of bodywork, or challenges such as slacklining or juggling (though it may be wise to avoid tightrope walks over precipitous drops or fire juggling).

While psychedelic sacraments may be intended to deliberately knock us off balance (and into new states of awareness), practitioners may wish to explore physical balance as an outward expression of their inner psychological state. By finding our physical balance (for example on a unicycle) and being 'in flow' within the psychedelic space, we may achieve acts of personal transformation, healing, and illumination.

Here is an example of movement practice that makes use of the four compass directions and the four inter-cardinal points in a ritual space. This approach combines physical activity with visualisation and the opportunity to magically intervene in the web of relationships within which the psychonaut exists. It can be used as a solitary or group practice with or without the use of sacred medicines.

Weaving the Web of Wyrd

Formally mark the beginning of the ritual by simply ringing a bell, or another more elaborate process.

Stand in the centre of the space in mountain asana (feet together, arms by the sides). Spend a moment being aware that you are both your own narrative as a 'self' moving through space and time and also that your 'self' emerges out of the relationships (from the biochemical to social levels and beyond) in which you live.

Using free-form movement or dance (with or without an instrument such as a rattle or background music) begin to move round the space. As you circle around, dancing and moving, bring your attention to the powers, symbolism and seasons of the year (or other concepts) you associate with each direction. These may be the eight festivals of the Pagan ritual year, the eight forms of Ganesha, the eight circuit model of Timothy Leary or something else. Your circle is emblematic of the universe you inhabit.

As you pass each direction of the circle, listen to what comes up for you. In a certain place you may find your attention drawn to loved ones, to projects you're engaged with, to difficulties you or others are experiencing, or other impressions.

As you move round the circle begin to see that you are in fact inside the 'Web of Wyrd', and that you are a 'technician of the sacred' in this space. Use your arms, legs and gestures, sound and words, to cut, plait, smooth and spin the lines of synchronicity and magic in the way that you Will (try to see or feel these relationships as though they were actual threads, tendrils or psychedelic tracers). As you move round the space your body becomes the shuttle on the loom, the weaver of magical change, interacting within this symbolic envelope (the eight directions) with the issues that arise in your awareness. You are the magician making changes in this model of reality (knowing that; As Above, So Below).

Once you feel that you have brought these threads of possibility into a new harmonious state, slow down your circumambulations and come to stand again in the centre. Be still for a moment and let what you have done sink in.

Make a prayer of thanks, or in some other way recognise and celebrate the transformative power of the universe.

Let your breathing come back to normal, ring a bell or use another ceremonial act to mark the end of the practice.

Gestures

Ritual gestures are used in every human culture. From shaking hands to Crossing oneself in Christian or Qabalistic ritual, pressing the palms together in prayer, through to the mudras of yoga and the magical passes of shamans. By investigating these symbolic movements, the psychonaut may discover useful techniques that can be used when high to help re-centre the bodymind, anchor specific mental states or insights, and for a range of other purposes.

In a group, holding hands—especially at the beginning and end of ceremonies—is always nice. This act is a symbol of the unity and trust between people who intend to travel through the psychedelic experience together.

Movements that link participants together can have a powerful effect when used in a ritual context, encouraging the group to breathe at a similar rate and develop a shared awareness.

Various mirrored movements or shared actions can be built into psychedelic ceremony. For instance while sitting in a circle holding hands, a pulse (made by squeezing the hand of the person next to you and them passing this grip on to the person on their other side) can be started that circulates through the group. This pulse may be used as a focus of attention; perhaps speeding up with the intention of generating psychic power within the group mind for particular purpose.

At the end of a ceremony participants can link hands, and then slowly raise them while stepping either towards or away from each other. Combined with a rising sound this gesture can be used to symbolically send the power of the ceremony outward and formally close the session. As the hands reach up and are released the experience (or 'energy') of the ceremony is offered to the wider world.

Sensuality and Sexuality

There are numerous ways to explore sensuality, sexuality and sacramental substances.

Massage, both giving and receiving, is a process that can blend wonderfully with drugs. This may range from an informal shoulder rub in the chill-out tent at a dance festival, through to more structured healing or ceremonial bodywork.

The cuddle puddle is an example of a sensual group activity. Rules for the level of intimacy are agreed before the session and members of the group then lay on the (full of cushions or similar) floor, in close contact with each other.

The group touch, embrace, non-sexually stoke, and provide close human contact with each other. The aim is to create a freeing, affirming, safe, fun and deeply human sense of warmth and care.

More erotic or playful versions of the cuddle puddle technique might include the use of oil, slime, mud or other liquids designed to increase the sensual nature of the experience (these methods combine very well with some of the phenethylamine family, notably 2C-B).

Drugs can be used to enhance and explore a variety of sexual activities from autoerotic explorations to orgiastic or sensual group activities. (D.M.Turner recommends trying to have an orgasm while taking 5-MeO-DMT while acknowledging that getting the timing right can be tricky.)

Obviously when using these techniques care must be taken to ensure that consent is properly given, that boundaries are respected, and that people are never pressured to engage in behaviours that they may not be comfortable with. This is especially true when powerful psychoactive drugs are being used which, because of their ability to loosen boundaries, may lead to difficulties in defining competence and consent.

The rules that govern adult erotic play (in S&M, BDSM and related contexts) should be observed so that sexual entheogenics are conducted in a safe, sane and consensual manner. They provide clear structures, regardless of the type of physical contact engaged in, which transfers well to entheogenic situations if all are familiar with a few basic fundamentals. The practices, the 'scene' (or script for the ritual/ sex play), discussion of limits and so on should be had while sober. These should be clearly understood and remain respected while under the influence of drugs.

'Safe words' or a traffic light system can be used (for example a person who is being flogged (or licked or stroked or whatever) can say 'green' meaning 'go', 'amber' meaning 'proceed with caution' and 'red' meaning 'stop immediately'. Great care should be exercised when experimenting with any kind of restraining techniques such as rope bondage. It would be wise to be very familiar with this territory without drugs, before combining these techniques.

With these considerations in mind, intimate explorations while using psychedelics can be powerfully transformative, whatever form the sensual/sexual interaction takes. One should choose one's companion(s) wisely.

Sex combined with drugs can be used to empower sigils (see page 86) and to perform other magical acts. Symbols may be drawn onto the body of one's lover/s and these are worn off, and by analogy sent into the unconscious mind/astral realm, as the erotic fun unfolds.

Some drugs will change the physiological sexual responses (e.g. erectile function or secretion of vaginal lubrication) and other aspects of bodily competence (creating for example tremors, loose bowels, or reduced co-ordination). A careful approach to dosage, noticing the point in the trip where sex may or may not 'work', and the use of aphrodisiac drugs can offset any limitations caused by a particular sacrament.

Sequential attention can become hard to maintain on some

psychedelics (such as medium to large doses of MDMA) and this may mean that genitally focused sex is less rewarding than sensual stroking and kissing.

Women may wish to investigate how their relationship with entheogens may change in relation to their menstrual cycle; anecdotal reports suggest that some might experience greater or lesser effects as hormones rise and fall.

Other physical acts, such as cutting the skin, piercing, tattooing etc. can also be explored, by the advanced practitioner, alongside the use of sacred medicines.

Animal Forms

It is useful to explore many forms of movement within the psychedelic state. Many martial arts systems use the movements of non-human animals to inspire their techniques. The idea of incorporating or being 'possessed' by an animal spirit is common in many shamanic traditions. Moving like a non-human animal is a way to summon and then embody the actual or imagined qualities of the creature in question. Using sound and movement to incarnate as an animal form, particularly a creature that the psychonaut feels some type of affinity with is a powerful technique.

Encounters with animal spirits (or 'allies') can happen spontaneously or be generated by internal imaginative techniques such as the innerworld or 'shamanic journey'. In this approach the intention is set (to meet the animal spirit), the basic format of the journey is understood in advance by the participant but no words are used to direct the experience.

Hunting for a Power Animal

A drum is playing. Hard rapid beats. There are no words given by the shaman but I am clear about the specifics of the journey.

"Listen to the drum", she had said. "Listen to the drum and it will take you to a doorway. Go through this and into the place beyond.

There you will find an animal to be your guide."

In my mind's eye there is a crack in the bark at the base of a tree. A tiny fairy house lined with emerald moss which folds backwards into a dark interior. I become small (or perhaps the aperture has grown great) and travel (by flying?) through this tunnel.

There is a brief view of a starry sky. (Perhaps indicating the many worlds this crack in reality can give me access to?) Then I find myself looking across a misty river with still quicksilver water.

There stands a heron, alert and single legged. Beak poised, shrouded in a robe of grey feathers, and I know I have come here to meet this magical animal. This bird represents my aspiration and my soul, the symbol of my nature.

Then the drumbeat changes and the vision fades, like coming up from the water I return to the surface. The floor hard beneath me, the blanket over me. I sense that I have found an important piece of (or process in) the jigsaw puzzle of my identity.

Internal Journeys

Guided imagery processes can be pre-recorded, or read aloud, while tripping. Such an 'inner journey' could be a central part in a more-or-less formalised ritual practice, or it might simply be something that is used by a group of friends, returning from a night out clubbing to get an ecstatic spiritual hit.

There are many ways such a journey could be structured; one might create a simple story (travelling through a wood, emerging in a clearing to discover something before returning to wakefulness) or, a more complex text drawing on symbolism that makes sense to the listener (a variation of this technique is 'pathworking' which uses the complex symbolism of the Hermetic Qabalah).

Here are two examples of guided imagery texts. The first is a story, using predominantly the language of science that aims to inspire a sense of awe and wonder in the listener. The second text is a journey to find a symbol in the unconscious mind in order to affect an unspecified act of personal transformation.

Guided imagery journeys, when performed live, are best read with a slow, sonorous voice and often feature a repeated refrain to enhance the induction of trance vision. A skilled practitioner reading a text will judge the audience and know when to slow down or pick up the pace (they do this by being sensitive to any movements, speed of breathing and other subtle clues from those on the journey).

Pre-recorded music, live percussion or other instruments can be used to provide additional sounds to support the journey.

Sitting in a comfortable chair or lying down allows the participant to forget their body and concentrate on the journey. Low light levels and closed eyes also help direct the attention inward.

At the end of these practices a bell may be rung, or the music may change in some way to help bring those following the journey to return to a more wakeful state.

A Meditation on Life, Death and Breath

Breathe in and out, listen to the sound, be aware of this feeling, this movement that slips between conscious and unconscious awareness. We can control how we breathe, sharp and shallow or deep and slow. Yet breath continues to work when we are fast asleep; we can make this process one we are aware of, or just let it do its thing without our attention.

The breath moves in, the breath moves out.

As we breathe here, we're going to weave a spell, a spell of awe, of amazement, of awareness. Listen, and let me tell you a story, to weave an enchantment by words to help us remember the way in which the breath, our breath, connects us to the entire universe. For, as magicians are apt to explain—as above so below; as within so without.

As we breathe, let's begin by noticing a simple and unassailable fact. That each breath in is like that very first breath you took when you were born. Emerging from the womb into the light, there was that moment when we escaped from the reality we knew while we were growing. A warm world of fluid, vibrating to the twin drum beats of our own heart and that of our mother. Our skin slick with vernix, our guts stoppered with meconium. A world of deep red light and sound waves penetrating the amniotic liquid from what you now recognise was the outside world.

From this organic cave each one of us emerges, and breathes. We suck in the air for the first time as a sudden transformation takes place. We have grown from our root, our navel. Attached by a living cord to our dark twin, the placenta, that gathers nourishment from our mother's blood and feeds us while we drift in our pre-birth state. Then, we open our mouths for air as we are born. Hormonal changes during labour slow, then stop, the production of fluid in the lungs, and initiate its reabsorption. Physical stimulation and handling during delivery encourages our baby self to breathe.

We need to work very hard to take our first breath, and our first few gasps may be shallow and irregular. But with each breath after birth, more air accumulates in our lungs, making it easier to breathe. Soon our breath becomes deeper and established. This rhythm will be our lifelong companion.

In and out.

A blood vessel close to our heart begins to close when we are newly born. Before birth this duct diverts blood away from the lungs. Once we begin our extrauterine life, blood begins to circulate through our lungs, and this structure retreats and closes during the first or second day of life. Our root changes from navel to mouth, through which we are now nourished and through which we have gasped that first breath.

This transition from fetal to adult circulation can take minutes or hours, and this transition is something we have all achieved. We breathe in, and in doing so we remember that first breath. That first visible transformation; where we became independent living entities, a transformation driven by unconscious processes, the ancient biological heritage of our species.

Breathe in. This is the breath of life.

Let us for a moment consider the backstory of this breathing body.

A few edited highlights of our 21st century genesis runs something like this:

Some three seconds after the universe expanded following the Big Bang it cooled to a state where subatomic particles assembled into atoms. Hydrogen atoms formed first, since they are the simplest type, the primal matter of existence. Cut to around 300 million years later *and the force of gravity, that love of mass for mass, had begun to gather the hydrogen into vast clouds that fell in on themselves, coalescing and condensing. As these clouds grew in size, the compression at the centre increased, hundreds of billions of times the pressure of our planet's atmosphere.*

13.2 billion years ago, this is when the stars turned on.

As they burnt their hydrogen fuel these stars became, through the immaculate conception of physics, countless pregnant seed heads that burst, releasing a strange cargo into vast space. From these ancient supernovae emerge the elements. Forged in the fusion fires of titanic nuclear furnaces, as the ancient stars grew heavy, expanding and exploding, they scattered new matter through the cosmos. From this nucleosynthesis hydrogen begat helium, helium begat carbon, carbon begat oxygen. Stars a little more massive than our sun form iron cores by this process. Heavy elements are produced by flaming orbs orders of magnitude bigger, where gold and lead are liberated by the supernova and smeared across the sky in thunderous detonation.

The periodic table is the record of these innumerable lights; uncountable gatherings of hydrogen formed at the Great Beginning, squeezing together and opening out. Breathing in, and out, and in doing so making all the worlds, the whole universe.

Such is the stuff that we are made of. From whale to woodlouse, our bodies quite literally come from the core of the stars.

Everything in the universe is made this way, from the alchemy of the stars. All matter.

Let's come a little closer to home, closer to our star-spun bodies that in this moment breathe in and out. For, as we are children of the stars we are also the children of the sun.

That splendiferous star that our world is circling right now is a third of a million times greater than the mass of our Earth.

We humans, along with most of the life on this world, have evolved to derive our nourishment from our star. The sun powers the cycle of photosynthesis which, in the time of ancient earth, turned our atmosphere from a carbon dioxide and methane mix into the oxygen rich environment that animates our bodies and makes our sky blue. It is this ability of life to capture sunlight that makes our species possible. That makes you and me possible.

Every second our Sun burns up 600 million tons of hydrogen, converting this into a million times the amount of energy used each year by humanity.

The photons emitted from the Sun's vast mass take only nine minutes to reach us across the 92-million-mile gap. But that light has been ricocheting around within our star for many tens of thousands, perhaps millions of years. Some of the photons are even older; particles of the light which we shall open our eyes to tomorrow morning were formed at the dawn of life on Earth.

Breathe in this power of the sun, the source of our existence.

Impossibly old star stuff comes together to form us, creatures that in turn feed from the power generated by the sun. Halfway through its lifespan, our star has a story that will go on this like this for another 5 billion years but we humans who know this—each one of us, breathing here—knows too that our lifespans are much, much shorter.

Breathe out, and know that as you are hearing this, you are dying.

The little knot of energy in the universe that constitutes you is fast winding down. Each breath we take is one closer to that final exhalation.

Watched from the perspective of evolutionary time our own little life is a tiny fluttering of biology. Watched through the eyes of geological time we hardly register at all. Compared to the titanic entropic droop of a universe stumbling towards its inevitable heat death, we are as nothing. Yet we certainly feel ourselves to be something. On the immediate scale of our humanity our death looms large. No culture fails to speak of death. No religion fails to speak about what death means, how it should be prepared for and, critically, what comes after death.

But whatever religious, scientific or cultural paradigm we inhabit the fact is that our breath out is like our final breath. And it is undeniable that our final breath is coming, inexorably closer.

Our bodies, no longer sustained by animating air, begin to decay after only minutes. The molecules that we are made from, their elements created in those ancient long-dead stars, will one day unravel, becoming the raw matter from which new forms of life may arise. But in reality this 'death', these changes, are happening as a continual process. As we breathe the cells within us replicate, entering the complex chemical dance of our organism and, in time, fade away. Our bodies are always in this state of flux, being nourished, living and dying. Our own death, while so significant to ourselves and those whom we love, is just another transformation. The energy structures that were 'us' become the 'other', and in turn these 'others' become 'selves' once more.

The breaking down of forms that is our death is no more surprising than the fact that stars eventually burn up. The whole of the biological network of our planet is a sequence of these lives and death, these transformations and revivifications. As above, so below.

At the scale of our bodies, blood cells are eliminated by built-in cell death, balancing their production in the bone marrow. The caspase enzyme, engine of programmed cell death that dwells in many of our cells, provides a mechanism by which damaged and potentially dangerous cells can be eliminated for the good of the organism as a whole. We die daily, millions upon millions of our cells. When our 'death' comes, that final out breath, if we have been blessed with the opportunity to grow old, none of the atoms in that body will be the ones we were born with. We are, and were, and shall be transformed.

This knowledge may not stop us fearing death, or grieving; these are natural human processes.

But it does help us see death as part of a larger story, as part of the narrative of the life force, the Great Mystery of which we are a part.

For this is the wonder of it all.

Here in this universe, despite its apparent hurtling towards entropy like an unstoppable juggernaut, we find that matter rises up into complexity and consciousness. That at every moment this awakening happens, as new processes that we call 'lives' emerge, ever changing, ever renewed. Perhaps this knowledge might remind us to live both as though we were going on forever and, at the same time, as though any moment now we are going to be gone—transformed.

Breathing in, and out.

(Now hold the hands of the people next to you; or, clasp your own hands.)

Feel the warmth of your skin, warmth derived from the great conflagration that is the Sun around which our Earth rotates. This warmth that is generated by a structure, a body, whose matter was forged in the aeons old fires of long dead stars. Feel that warmth that shall one day pass from the thing we identify as 'ourselves'. Know that this warmth, this life happens because of the wonderful fact that physics gives rise to chemistry, chemistry to biology, and biology to awareness. And even as this warmth passes from the selves we are, it is transformed and rises again into new living flesh.

Be aware, as you breathe, of this breath of life and of death and the endless cycle, a cycle that is perhaps repeated on innumerable other worlds in our universe. For though we may be the first, or perhaps the last, it is likely that out there in the stars there are other planets like us, throbbing with life, and most likely with death too.

Breathe in this sublime knowledge, this awesome reality.

Breathe out this endless possibility.

Breathe.

Stalking Power

This is a guided visualisation for finding a power object. This imagined object might be used for healing, transformation or another purpose. The object may be anything that is presented in the vision, a landscape, an animal, a person, a cultural product or symbol.

The text is designed so that it can be read slowly, perhaps with the use of background music or other effects. The language is deliberately vague so that the scenes described are open to a variety of interpretations.

Feel your body resting on the floor. Feel the weight of your form, just resting, held easily and relaxed.

Feel the weight of your bones, your muscles, your skin, your whole body, your whole being, dropping down easily and without any worry, into the depths of the earth.

Drifting down, down, down into the rich, wise earth.

Now imagine that you go so deep that you find yourself lying down in a cave. In your imagination, open your eyes and look at this cavern, stand up and explore the space.

[Allow time for participants to make this transition to their 'astral body' and move around the space they have discovered.]

Now you see a doorway, one that you had not spotted before. You know that behind this door is a magical object. A symbol of your power to transform yourself and our situation in the waking world.

Open this door and move beyond it. And find your power object.

[Pause again.]

Get to know that object and know your connection with it.

Now, with what you have discovered, you return to the doorway.

Pass through this into the cave beyond and rest again on the good earth.

Feel your power object with you and keep it with you as, in the vision, you close your eyes and allow your body to rise magically up, up towards the surface.

Coming up, and up, knowing that this powerful symbol of transformation is with you, yours to use in whatever way you need.

Up and up until you are aware that you are lying on the earth again, in your waking body.

Feeling the life force in your body, your bones and muscles and skin.

Feeling relaxed and aware and inspired you are back to your waking self, out of the vision and here again.

Open your eyes.

Adventures in the Ultraworld

There are of course many interesting things one can do whilst high, ranging from playful pursuits through to more challenging practices. Some of these activities can be thought of as games, others as praxiological forms of spiritual enquiry, and still others as acts of magic.

Artistic Explorations

Drawing, painting, body painting, writing and many other artistic practices are wonderful things to do when you are high.

Psychedelics provide us with an opportunity to play with paint, draw in the sand or mould clay in a way where we can reconnect to a child-like appreciation of exploration and fun without self-critical judgements about making 'good' art or a specific final product.

During trips focused on inner exploration, creating artworks may have a powerful transformative effect. Drawings could be made at different points throughout a trip, expressing changing psychedelic insights in visual form. These pictures may be used for post-trip meditation and reflection, as anchors for realisations reached during the experience, and as talismanic, magical images.

Consuming Content

Since entheogens make us very sensitive to set and setting, consuming media such as film and TV in these states needs to be carefully considered. Nevertheless, there are many films that have been specifically designed to be very engaging when approached from the psychedelic state.

Generally, movies without a complex narrative make for the best drug-enhanced viewing where there is plenty of cognitive 'space' for the tripper to make sense of what is going on in their own way. Beautiful scenes of landscapes, animated art or dance can make for great viewing when high.

It can be interesting to make your own film and/or audio recordings while tripping. The psychonaut can then reflect on the trip from another perspective when back at baseline and the recordings may provide raw media for future artistic experiments.

Wonderful Things

Psychedelics work by creating enhanced connectivity within the brain; this means that the simplest object can become pregnant with meaning.

Experiment with holding or otherwise encountering objects that are significant to you. Everyday objects can become the locus for astonishing, ramifying insights (such as in the probably entheogenic ritual at ancient Eleusis when a blade of barley was presented to the initiate as 'the seed of wisdom').

Try slowly, mindfully, eating a piece of fruit while considering all the connections between your body and the people, animals and plants that have brought this food to your life. In your imagination follow the biological web that evolved into this moment of nourishment.

Likewise look at your hands and all the things around you and allow the psychedelic awareness to spread out to encompass the totality of connections—physical, biological, social and spiritual.

Lie down on the earth and bring your attention to the fact of your weight and how the ground holds you up. Below you is the molten core of our planet, above you the vastness of interstellar space.

Sculpts

Sculpts provide a form of artistic process that can be very helpful when using psychedelic drugs. A term borrowed from psychology, a sculpt can be made from many things; people, words written on slips of paper, tarot cards, random found objects in either the landscape or the home, or many other ways. By arranging these objects in a space (which could be anything from a table top to a whole room) the psychonaut is able to explore the relationships that the objects represent. These could be family relationships, influences on the practitioner, philosophical ideas or any other set of interactions they want to explore. One of the objects in the sculpt usually represents the self of the practitioner.

From an initial configuration, which reflects current patterns, items can be moved and, by analogy (or sympathetic magic) this mirrors the changes the psychonaut wishes to manifest in that network of relationships. As objects are moved closer or further away from each other, removed or augmented with new objects, so the transformation takes place. This is a means of using a symbolic language within the setting of the psychedelic journey to reprogram the inner set of the practitioner and perhaps create magically wrought changes in the outer, apparent world.

The creation and maintenance of a ceremonial altar can be imagined as a type of sculpt.

Cut-ups

A cut-up is made by literally cutting up a narrative, then randomly rearranging the pieces; sometimes with subsequent deliberate changes. This technique can be applied to images, text, sound or other materials. This method can be employed to explore synchronistic and serendipitous connections within the mind of the practitioner and to generate new ideas.

Such creations are usually made fairly rapidly to prevent too much conscious deliberation. Reflecting on the content thus created, while in the psychedelic state or after the drugs have worn off, can stimulate interesting insights.

Playing Games

For fun, to stimulate creativity and to provide illuminating insights, there are plenty of linguistic and physical games that can be played while high. Try various parlour games; such as the memory testing The Tray Game (or 'Kim's Game'), the deductive 20 Questions, or the surreal 'Mornington Crescent'. Deliberately 'crazy' conversations and verbal exploration of koans (such as the classic 'what is the sound of one hand clapping?') can prove fascinating while in psychedelic space.

Physical games such as Twister, and sports from Frisbee to surfing are worthwhile exploring (while of course being mindful of health and safety) when high on drugs. On psychedelics the tendency to discern meaning in even (apparently) trivial events can make these practices more than just amusing ways for a group to spend time together. Games such as the 'levitation' of people ('light as a feather, stiff as a board') and stage magic tricks can be both entertaining and can help psychonauts explore the limits of perceived reality within the psychedelic space.

The Superheroes Game

This is an example of an enjoyable practice that can lead to deep insights, especially when played while high. It arose spontaneously from a group of friends sat around one day and serves as an exemplar of communal verbal play. This game works in interpersonal environments where a degree of linguistic competence, empathy and focused attention is possible (e.g. medium or low doses of MDMA, towards the end of an LSD trip and/or with the support of cannabis).

Participants (at least three, and generally no more than ten or so) sit in a circle. The first player describes in turn the superpowers they imagine the other players possess. These powers should be linked to actual (or perceived) attributes of each person.

For example; 'I think Bob's superpower is emotional x-ray vision because he's so good at seeing how people are really feeling and responding positively to that', or 'Natasha's superpower is that she can make everyday things magical because as a dancer she uses gravity and the human body to create art', or 'Dan's power is that of a Jovial god, because he's great at encouraging other people to be magnificent and confident and he's always inviting us to awesome parties like this one!' etc.

Once the first participant has gone round the group naming what they think each person's superpower could be, they explain what their own superpower is to the group. The next person takes their turn to name the powers of the all other members in the group, including their own. The game progresses until everyone has taken a turn.

Psychogeography

Going on a journey, especially a walk, is an excellent thing to do while high on psychedelics. There is a natural relationship between the metaphorical trip of the drug and the literal trip in a physical landscape.

There are numerous ways to approach such a journey, depending on the environment and the sacred medicines available. Substances may be deployed at specific points in the journey (such as short acting psychedelics) and/or the journey may be made while under the influence of a longer lasting sacrament.

Practices such as creating shrines, leaving offerings, making art from found objects, taking photographs, inscribing symbols, talking with the spirits of place, and many other ways to interact with the environment can be employed by the psychogeographical psychonaut.

Different ways of moving (e.g. very slow walking, running, crawling etc.) can be used to alter perception and, alongside the use of drugs, provide the voyager with new perspectives on both inner and outer landscapes. One example would be to walk quickly up a hill, keeping the eyes downcast and focused on the path. At the summit the traveller looks up for the first time, surveying the wide world all around. Be playful and silly too! Enjoy the space, explore and be curious. If you are concerned that you 'look weird' find a place to be where you are not easily observed or create a cover story about your behaviour (which you may only need in your own head to make you less anxious).

Objects may be taken from one place along the path and moved to another. This may be imagined to have some symbolic meaning, connecting together different aspects of the journey and the self.

Wild foods (leaves, berries, flowers etc.) may be consumed during the expedition if they are available. These may be imagined as brimming with 'vital chi' and conferring particular blessings or powers. Many symbolic and magical interactions may unfold between the psychonaut, and the plants and animals encountered during the trip.

Paying attention to the sights, sounds, smells and other sensations of the journey is an important part of any psychogeographic process and so if a walk is made in the company of other people chit-chat is generally kept to a minimum.

The walk may be pre-planned along a known path or could feature the random selection of a route characteristic of a situationist dérive. Randomising methods (such as a coin or dice) may be employed to choose which direction to go. Such a journey can be seen as being analogous to an exploration of the hidden aspects of the self: as the psychogeographer is walking a new path through the landscape, so too are they discovering novel routes through the psyche.

Many psychedelics increase visual acuity. In higher doses the morphing shapes and visuals characteristic of many substances may make it difficult to see, while at lower doses these substances can be useful aids in spotting previously unnoticed features in the landscape (such as simulacra and wild animals). Spend some time being still and see what you notice. Observe slow moving snails feeding in tidal pools by the ocean, watch closely as an insect climbs the titanic structure of a grass stem. Take the time to listen, to smell the air, to feel that grass beneath your feet.

Psychogeographic walks can also be psychedelic pilgrimages or 'hunts' (in the sense that the Wixáritari people hunt the 'blue deer' of the peyote cactus). When searching for wild mushrooms or other drug plants it is common practice to consume a small amount of the target plant when it is initially found in order to help the hunter 'tune in' to the spirit they are seeking.

Museum Level

The term 'museum level' describes a dosage of any substance that allows the user to successfully enjoy a public space (such as a museum, gallery, botanic garden or similar) in an altered state of awareness. Dosage needs to be carefully calculated so that the subject passes as behaving normally to other people. Museums, which usually offer a fairly unstructured environment, where it is expected that visitors will spend periods silently contemplating objects on display, or excitedly talking about exhibits, are ideal locations for tripping.

Careful consideration of set and substance can allow the psychonaut to successfully explore any number of wonderful places. As well as museums, entheogens can also be deployed when visiting other historic sites, landscapes, art installations, firework displays and so on.

More intense environments, such as music concerts, theatre, political or sporting events where large crowds are present, religious festivals and gatherings, funfairs and theme parks can also be explored while high. It may be wise to use lower doses in some of these contexts and/or to have one person in the party who opts to take a lower dose (or nothing at all) and act as 'tour guide'.

A Visit to the Psychedelic Museum

The entrance to the museum is brilliant white. Outside it's a glorious summer's day and bright light streams through the windows high in the domed ceiling. My sunglasses obscure the fact that my pupils are hugely dilated (especially in this brilliant chamber). I check my coat and bag into the cloakroom, pay for my ticket but decide I don't want to use, at least for this visit, the electronic methods of gallery interpretation on offer. I push my phone safely into my pocket and head inside.

The entheogen I have taken makes the rippling carving around the doorway even more impressive than the last time I visited. This is the entrance to The Psychedelic Museum, which I'm entering at 'museum level', that is, while moderately high.

Of course this museum, like any 'shrine of the muses' (which is what 'museum' literally means) is perfect for exploring while in an altered state. For, while some places aim for either a fine-art gallery feel (with one of two star objects in glass cases), a panoply of digital interactive elements, or 'old school' style plan chests full of mysterious and wonderful things—the Psychedelic Museum, attempting to reflect the multiple perspectives of the psychedelic experience, includes all three museological approaches.

Moreover, this museum blends spaces together, blurring boundaries and styles. I enter the main hall through a short dark tunnel, illuminated with famous quotes that appear, in glowing letters and then fade away, creating a web of words that tune in nicely with the visual changes I'm starting to get. 'If the doors of perception were to be cleansed...' and, 'we're not dropping out here, we're infiltrating and taking over'.

The collection contains many fascinating items and whenever I've visited, I've seen something different. This is probably because one of the features of the museum is that they frequently move the artefacts around. In fact, just as I arrive into the hall (the museum is really one large space, with various more or less delineated zones created by moveable walls and other elements) I see a large white rabbit bobbing along. It's being transported by three members of staff (easy to spot in their black clothes and t-shirts sporting the logo of the psychedelic museum). The crew gently stand the rabbit which, judging by the way they are handling it must be made of ceramic, atop a small plinth. Two workers stand back to regard the display, calculating I assume some arcane museum aesthetics of position. The third adjusts a light that illuminates the giant watch-peering bunny. On closer inspection I can see a label: 'This White Rabbit was gifted to The Psychedelic Museum by The Psychedelic Society, Birmingham 2020'. There's an electronic tag on the plinth where I could access more information but I've got enough to think about here. The rest of the label is suitably gnomic reading; "You may be early, you may be late or you may be right on time". Obviously, because I'm on drugs, I interpret the arrival of this totemic psychopomp of psychedelia as a good omen.

I can feel the medicine now, very clearly. I've come up and am likely to plateau now for about two hours. Plenty of time to explore this magical space. The weather is fine and it's early in the day, later I'll be able to come down gently in the delightful psychedelic garden attached to the museum, then find my way to the centre of the building and 'The High Tea Shop', there to lounge on a chaise and listen to the wonderful range of psychedelic music (from The Incredible String Band through to early recordings of Siberian spirit songs) until closing time. Drinking chai and, if I'm in the mood, writing about my journey for this book.

Spreading through me there is openness and wonder and I sense that I need to be gentle with myself. This is a recreational and nourishing visit, not one where I want to test my psyche in any way. With this in mind I decide not to step past the 'hazard' tape and into the gallery that holds some of the more difficult parts of the collection. There are some challenging objects there, documents and artefacts from the era of military experimentation with LSD. There is a mock-up of a Porton Down acid research cell (featuring a video of historian Andy Roberts, speaking at break-neck speed about this darker side of the British acid story).

But everywhere else in the museum isn't just sweetness and light. I find myself at one point fascinated by a slideshow of photographs in a case devoted to the use of peyote (a substance in the same chemical family as the one I'm on right now). Amongst the amazing beadwork, feathered shamans' hats, and elaborately decorated robes, a rolling series of photographs are projected onto a white Huicholi costume. These include images of animal sacrifice, an important part of the tradition in that part of Mexico, and (having gone through the inner dialogue about meat eating, animal cruelty and so on) I find myself fascinated by how I feel both empathy for the slaughtered goats, and an understanding of the Huicholi people who are simply including the preparation of food into their spiritual tradition. I find myself wondering at the beauty of brilliant red splashed across pristine white cloth.

Museum visits are often like this for me, especially when I'm high. I feel like I'm seeing multiple interpretations of each object. Not getting fixed in any one story (which is perhaps a key effect of psychedelics).

There are notices of appreciation as I wander around, thanking members of the international psychedelic community for their generous donations and loans; this is place is truly a collaborative work, and a literal wonderland.

I find myself beside a case of objects donated by the estate of Richard Evans Schultes; Shipibo textiles and faded field notes about the presence of 'telepathin' in ayahuasca. I peer at each of the objects in turn. There are ancient stone cups made for holding the jungle brew. There's even a tiny star shaped box (perhaps a donation from one of the Daime churches?) affixed to the outside of the glass case beneath which a label reads 'smell me!' (looping back to my Alice in Wonderland moment at the entrance). So I do. Yes, that's it! The unmistakable scent of the rainforest potion, Ha! The smell of ayahuasca in the morning. I chuckle; smells like victory!

On a nearby wall a circular film screen shows the preparation of ayahuasca. The movie has been shot from above and I'm looking straight down into a boiling cauldron of brown liquid as figures with a range of skin tones and hairstyles, stir and chop and stoke the fire. Then the picture changes and now I'm presented with film of a Santo Daime ceremony. Initially this is also shot from above, but as I watch the camera pulls back and down and it is though I am standing shoulder to shoulder with the members of the white clothed congregation. The sound of singing "Guiado pela Lua e pelo Sol" (previously very distant, possibly generated by speakers under the floor) swells and I can hear it clearly. The rattles and drums in the cases beside me seem to vibrate as the sound builds. Then, after what feels like ages but was perhaps only a few moments, it softens and fades into a gentle background rhythm.

I wander on, deeper into the collection. There is a dome shaped structure with dance music playing where UV banners from Megatripolis and Burning Man hang, incandescent with black light. Beyond this there is a full-scale replica of the laboratory of Alexander Shulgin (a delicate collection of the enigmatic flasks, retorts and test tubes in which Sasha cooked up his psychedelic alchemy). In one display case is his lab book, a stained grimoire of chemical conjuration. I linger here for a while, entranced by an original Alex Gray painting of Alexander and Ann hanging, self-referential and glowing, in the recreated lab.

Here I make my connection, between the sacrament I have taken and this story. Again I feel as though I sense all of it, all the aspects of MDMA and its sister medicines. I am surrounded by objects that hold me in a network of narratives; of Goa Gil and the emergence of psytrance, of the tragic death of Leah Betts, of the early explorations of MDMA in psychotherapy, the period of its banning and the 'Ecstasy destroys monkey brains' propaganda, through 'til now, when MDMA has returned as a legitimate therapeutic agent and is available to licensed non-medical users.

I sit for a moment, surrounded by this web of meaning and possibility and give thanks for the truth that in many places in the world we are finding better ways to be with the existence of these miraculous chemicals.

I'm gently coming down but it's still early in the afternoon. I make my way into the garden. There's an exhibition outside of rare datura plants co-curated by Kew Gardens. It's about the right time of year to admire those fantastical trumpeting flowers, and sit, and reflect on my trip thus far...

Vigils & Vision Quests

A stationary variant of the outdoor psychogeographic trip is that of undertaking a vigil. This process, known by names such as 'sitting out' or 'vision quest', generally assumes that the shaman will stay in one place for the duration of one night or longer.

In some traditions the vision quest becomes a powerful ordeal and initiation process. Several days and nights are spent outdoors in a remote wilderness, often within a small ritually demarcated area. The practitioner stays in this space and is periodically brought minimal food and water (often containing entheogens).

Vigils are usually solitary practices and generally take place in wild and remote locations, often overnight. Suitable clothing, especially in regions where the night-time temperature drops significantly, is important. For longer vigils it is useful to have another person as helper who will come to check on the practitioner and ensure that they are safe and bring whatever supplies have been agreed. Shorter vigils of one day or night, or even a few hours, can be revelatory in forcing the vision quester to remain still, thus seeing a different perceptual slice through time in a place. Our usual movements through the landscape allow at most a few minutes in one position, so the lifeforms of the area are not encountered unless by a fluke of timing. Sitting and watching expands our Now of being in a place, stretches the amount of interactions possible, and gives space for reflection upon the nuances of the environment. Just as looking at an artwork is a very different process when given adequate time for contemplation (say, a good half an hour), compared to the two minutes it takes to notice the obvious, basic components of a painting. Our world deserves more than the few seconds we usually take to look at it.

Raves

Going to a rave or party setting can be used an opportunity to deploy a variety of techniques which help transform a good night out into something outstanding, or even sacred and sublime. Using entheogenic technologies in these settings demonstrates that there need be no separation between fun and the spiritual endeavour.

Going raving will involve some amount of personal preparation (of costume, make-up etc.), and attention can be brought to this as both a pragmatic process (the desire to get ready and look great) as well as the symbolic meaning of cleansing and preparing for a psychedelic adventure. Particular choices of garments and accessories could be guided by their historical and emotional stories, as well as aesthetics. One might choose finger rings, for example, with certain associations, worn in combination.

The psychonaut may decide to throw or otherwise dedicate a party in honour of a particular intention, mythological character or concept. Suitable clothing, choice of location, foods, decoration, music etc. may reflect this intention.

Techniques such as chanting can be easily deployed while dancing, as can particular mudras and other symbolic gestures. Where there is a specific intention this can be sigilised or represented in some way and then obliterated during the party process. In the voudou tradition this is done by drawing a vevé (the magical symbol or seal) of a spirit on the floor of the ritual chamber (often in flour or salt). This is gradually erased as the dancing gets more exuberant. A similar technique may be employed where the dancing shaman has a rune, sigil or other symbol drawn on their body that is sweated off by frenetic dancing. The destruction of the sigil that represents the desire is analogous to the movement of the intention from its inert state as 'just a symbol' in consciousness, to its implanting in the deep mind or unconscious (where the magic happens).

Warriors Working

A British magician reflects on using the power of the dance floor to charge an act of magic:

> *"A notable series of rituals that were incredibly successful were based around the club scene; a friend and magical co-worker, fed up with losing his friends to AIDS, arranged the series as part of an assault on the HIV virus and the AIDS syndrome. With the club owner's permission, we would arrive at the club before the start of the main evening's festivities, create it as a sacred space with our initial ritual—using for instance a sigil in flour on the floor—then withdraw to change into ordinary clubbing gear for a few hours. At the peak of the night, we would reappear briefly on the dance floor in robes again. We were using the energies of psychedelics, dance and music, channelling some of the ecstasy of the rave into magickal effect. The results were truly impressive, including major remissions in individuals known to the team and an overall shift in how people viewed AIDS: no longer is it necessarily a death sentence and I believe our work contributed to that shift of perception."*

That "shift in perception" included, by coincidence or synchronicity if you prefer, the development of successful and accessible medicines to treat HIV.

Here is another example of blending the ceremonial 'spiritual' use of drugs with dance culture:

Rave Medicine

We are sitting in the maloca (the name of the ancestral house where people gather for ceremony in some Amazonian cultures). The building has canvass walls fastened over a framework of wooden posts. In the middle of the circular space burns a fire. The centre of the roof is open to the night sky, four great timbers, the main pillars of the maloca, stand at each corner of the hearth. Beside one of them is a container for the sacred medicine, San Pedro cactus, powdered into a fine, mescaline rich dust.

People are sitting and chatting, some playing instruments; there is an informal atmosphere. The shaman (our host) comes forward and welcomes us all to the space, to an evening that will combine ancient and modern ways of using this magical substance. He takes tobacco, rolled with a cornhusk and smokes it, blessing the gathering and the medicine. Other prayers are offered, and then it is time to take the cactus. We choose our own dose, powdered San Pedro taken dry with a water chaser or mixed together into a slurry and knocked back.

Some folk (there are about fifty people present in total) choose to remain by the fire in the maloca, playing guitars and drums and singing. The shaman invites the rest of us to the warehouse building on the site. Here the first of the evening's DJs are about to perform.

The large room is bedecked with glowing ultraviolet banners, laser lights split the haze produced by a smoke machine and burning incense. Shoes are removed and, as the medicine starts to come on, the dancing begins on the carpeted floor. In the corner of the room is an altar arranged with the symbols of the medicine path; feather fans decorated with beadwork, the horns of a deer and flowers. Along one wall there are cushions, space to sit and chat, or meditate or lie down and enter the visions of the cactus while bare-footed dancers gyrate to the pumping beats.

Outside this space, in the cool night air, there is a brazier around which folk can sit and smoke and chat. While cannabis and tobacco are being used by some present, an important feature of this gathering is that everyone is on the same psychedelic medicine and at very similar doses.

Returning to the maloca at around 2pm there are more prayers and medicine. Someone asks that as we dance we send our good *energy to those people suffering as refugees around the world. Cedar, a cleansing plant in some North American traditions, is sprinkled upon the fire. After the medicine is passed around the shaman plays with a laser, scattering its light through the smoke from the hearth, a glorious fusion of ancient and modern entheogenic culture. There is acoustic music, singing and gentle talking. One person is getting in touch with some powerful emotions (they are weeping) but there are others present to comfort them and, after a short time, they come forward to watch the flames and be blessed with cedar smoke, smiling again.*

Back to the dance floor, music progresses into deeper, harder psytrance. Then as dawn breaks the DJs change and gentler tunes are played to greet the day. Some people are dancing, other sleeping or doing yoga at the edges of the dance floor, still others slip away home. Everyone looks fresh faced, and while sleep will make extra demands later in the day, for now the mood is one of wakeful pleasure at the sublime fact of mere existence.

Festivals

Festivals oriented around the creative arts, particularly music, offer excellent (potentially optimum) settings for drug experimentation and exploration. Lighting, music and other environmental and cultural elements come together to produce beautiful, playful, diverse settings. Many festivals include explicitly spiritual elements (the ritual burning of The Man in the Mojave Desert or the fabulous Dance Temple created by Idanha-a-Nova lake to take two examples). A festival lasting a few days can provide a profound initiatory environment for the psychonaut, allowing time and space to move through many different experiences (and drugs).

Events such as raves and festivals can allow adults to reconnect with the importance of play. Playing with each other and with toys, from glow sticks to wild costumes, is an empowering process. Playful activity allows us to engage in an open-ended, exploratory activity that is the underpinning strategy by which humans learn. Play can be a true celebration of life and in that respect alone may constitute a spiritual practice. Play has many benefits to both the individual and the group; it is also, by definition, fun!

Most festivals include quieter areas for when the psychonaut wants time to chill out and reflect. Some festivals provide support for attendees who are experiencing challenging trips in the form of calming and safe environments with trained psychedelic guides. This is obviously of great benefit to the whole festival community.

Mindful Smoking

Tobacco is commonly employed in ritual smoking in many styles of shamanic ritual. This may be as part of a structured ceremony or in the more informal setting of a party, rave or festival event. Tobacco can serve to bring us back to the somatic level of the body, it can help straighten the explorer out after an intense psychedelic experience, or provide a pause, a punctuation mark in a trip that may be used to take the ceremony/experience in a new direction.

The use of smoke to offer prayers appears in numerous cultures. These may be prayers of thanksgiving and may also include elements of petition, asking for help from whatever gods, spirits or cultural constructs are believed in. Smoking any substance will create an almost immediate effect. This exhaled smoke might be imagined to carry some form of psychic impression from the person who has breathed it in (certainly bacteria and even our own DNA are carried in the air as we breathe out). Another person might breathe in exhaled smoke as part of a ceremony or it could be blown onto an object to consecrate it. Smoke can be used to flush out 'negative forces' and cleanse the aura of the patient during a shamanic style healing (in much the same way as smudging with sage or other herbs).

Here is an example of ritualised smoking practice:

Lighting a cigarette, the psychonaut breathes smoke upwards into the air, connecting to the spirits, forces or qualities imaged to be associated with the heavens. The tobacco, blunt, or other smoke is held between the index finger and thumb so that the lit tip points towards the smoker. If a pipe or chillum or other smoking method is used, another suitably ritualised way of holding the smoking device could be observed.

Another inhalation is taken and the smoke is breathed downwards upon the earth, honouring and linking with all the qualities of the earth and the underworlds. Another puff of smoke is directed to the left and to the right, bringing to mind the qualities of these directions. Alternatively smoke might be blown out and a hand used to waft it over the head and down across the shoulders and back. In this manner the ritualist is covered in all directions by the protective, sanctifying vapour. Another breath is taken and a puff of smoke is directed toward some symbolic object; if outside this is customarily the sun, moon, or another celestial source of light. Otherwise the breath is sent as an offering to Grandfather Fire (be that a hearth or lighted candle).

Once the directions have been honoured, the rest of the tobacco is smoked while prayers (verbalised or internal) are made. This may include statements of aspiration (oaths and Statements of Intent), requests for blessing and/or opportunities to give thanks for the blessings that the smoker enjoys (not least of which is the sacred herb being used in the rite). The cigarette is held as before, mindfully keeping the glowing end pointing towards the practitioner. The cigarette may of course be passed on to another person present who may repeat the self-blessing/orientation process (up, down, left, right and centre) before making other prayers. When being passed the cigarette may be presented in some slightly formalised way, with a word of blessing or some stylised ritual movement.

Handheld vaporisers or other devices could be used for this practice. These novel smoking technologies reduce the amount of particulate material and gases, such as carbon monoxide, that are present in combusted smoke. There may be health benefits to these methods of administration as well as the possibility of creating a rather more 'up' or 'lighter' high (because of reduced body load).

Sigils

A sigil is a representation of a desire (ranging from a personal wish through to a grand aspiration) encoded in a way that is often abstract or highly simplified. Many approaches to making sigils are described in the writing of British magician and artist Austin Osman Spare. Spare provides a variety of methods for generating sigils, ranging from the free form or associative, through to the more mechanistic method of creating a monogram formed from the letters of a magical statement of intent.

Though graphic sigils are the best known type, various other media can be used to create a sigil. For example; the letters in a written statement of intent could be associated with sounds and used to create music. Ritual intentions, spoken aloud and recorded, can be manipulated and the resultant drone-like audio used as backing music for psychedelic experiments. Sigils may be built from clay or other substances as three-dimensional forms. Sigils may be encoded into scent or other sensory modalities.

A sigil can be imagined as a symbol of intention that is unintelligible to the conscious mind, which is implanted using an altered state of awareness (in this context generated by magical medicines) into the unconscious (where it can magically change the self and/or universe). Imaginal energy and intent bring the sigil to life, empowering the desire it represents (e.g. by breathing power into the object while high, and visualising the sign glowing with magical energy).

Once charged the sigil may be ceremonially removed for awareness in a matter appropriate to the intention it represents. Sigils may be burnt to ashes, written on rice paper and eaten, buried, set adrift on a river etc. For some sigils the magician may wish to keep them in a conspicuous place (their home, workplace etc.) for some time, 'sending energy' into the sigil whenever they notice it.

Take your intention or aspiration. Encode it into a sigil, charge it with power (using a method that you enjoy and that 'feels right' in terms of the desire you are attempting to actualise) and then let it go. It's that simple.

Conversely a series of artworks, such as drawings, may be created (again while in an altered state of awareness so that there is little conscious deliberation) and a sigil might be discovered by looking for repeated motifs in the pictures created. This motif, once identified, is then taken to symbolise an important unconscious process. The emerging sigil is used as a focus for meditation and, eventually, its message may be consciously understood.

Mimetic Magic

Mimetic (also known as sympathetic) magic can be performed while under the influence of psychedelics. (Some magicians are of the opinion that the radically interconnected awareness created by psychedelics increases the effectiveness of this and other kinds of magic.)

Candle magic, where an enchantment is cast by staring at a candle (often made from wax, coloured according to some occult system of correspondence) is a simple and effective mechanism for mimetic spellcasting. A pin is pushed into the lighted candle and the mental association is made, 'when this pin drops the spell is cast and my intention manifests!' This type of mimetic link; 'as X happens so Y follows' is the basis of this style of enchantment.

Many aspects of ritual make use of this mimetic approach so that the meaning we ascribe to a ritual action is echoed by the world, both inner and outer.

The resourceful shaman or magician will have many such techniques up their mysterious sleeves and will be adept at employing these, often using found materials or situations, as required.

After a spell is cast magicians often suggest that it can be beneficial to take the attention elsewhere. This may mean breaking the set and setting by any number of means. This may include a banishing practice (which could be an elaborate ritual, or simply laughing to break the mood, a method developed within the Chaos Magic approach). One might end a spell casting session by leaving the room and going for a walk, or eating some food (to 'ground' the bodymind). By engaging in 'something else', the magician leaves the spell to do its work. A commonly employed analogy is that of planting a seed. After sowing the spell in the great interconnected Mystery of the universe, it is best to leave it alone and allow it to grow rather than dig it up again for examination with the conscious awareness.

Divination

There are many methods of divination, ranging from the complex (such as the calculations needed in astrology) to the instinctive (watching clouds and divining meanings from their shapes). At various points throughout a trip (typically towards the end) interesting divination experiments may be conducted.

The majority of divinatory practice is less about foretelling the future than it is about understanding the present. Through our use of tarot, I Ching or other methods we have an opportunity to reflect in a new way on the present. By externalising our thinking processes into a series of images or objects (cards, coins or whatever), and interacting with those symbols, often in the company of other people, we can discover novel approaches to understand our current situation and the options available to us. (This process is very similar to the use of sculpts described above). It is also the case, especially for experienced diviners, that information may arise through what appear to be parapsychological means. Such precognitive or inexplicable intuitions usually appear as flashes of insight.

The rapport provided by entheogens such as MDMA can be very useful when conducting divination sessions and in the hands of a skilled diviner can be used to discover a deep understanding of a situation, affecting therapeutic and other changes.

Diviners' tools such as black mirrors, crystal balls and scrying mirrors can be interesting to experiment with while in the psychedelic state (and also the hypnagogic state). It can be fun to listen to white noise on the radio for spirit messages, scry with bowls of liquid or look for insights in other chance events such as patterns in tea leaves or text found by opening a book at random.

For more experienced practitioners Ouija boards, summoning demons to get secret knowledge, possession mediumship, and other divinatory methods may also be interesting to explore when high on drugs.

Sensory Deprivation

Some entheogens work very successfully in 'silent darkness' (such as high doses of mushrooms, chewed *Salvia divinorum,* and ketamine) but sensory deprivation or restriction can be used in conjunction with many chemicals. This may be as simple as closing the eyes, or as elaborate as the use of floatation tanks, ganzfeld techniques or other methods for reducing sensory input.

Restriction of sensation may be built into a ritual practice of initiation, often acting as part of a stylised ordeal. Personal transformation is achieved by the release from this symbolic or actual constriction into liberation. Many initiation rituals into esoteric groups make use of this technique, for example blindfolding and binding the body with cords then removing these bonds as part of Wiccan or Masonic ceremony.

What follows is an example of a ritual using ketamine and sensory restriction. This ceremony demonstrates a fusion of elements characteristic of the esoteric approach known as Chaos Magic. Note how the structure of the rite, like all good entheogenic ceremonies, is designed to harmonise with the way the ketamine trip unfolds. There is the lead up to the experience supporting a specific set and creating a particular setting. The time between insufflation and the onset of the experience allows for the mummification process to be completed and the psychonaut to be laid down just as they fall into the K-hole and consciousness is extinguished. Silence is maintained while the psychonaut is unconscious and the rest of the rite is arranged to unfold as the 'I' of their awareness comes back online.

Temple K Initiation Rite

The setting is a warm and comfortable indoor space with blankets, furry cushions and the floor covered by mattresses. The ritual begins with the sharing of water.

Water is placed in a vessel and the three participants in the ceremony hold it between them. Together they say:

"This is the water of life. This is the water of life. This is the water of life".

One says, "All good spirits are here. All helpful forces. All beings are friendly to each other in this space". Softly the other two psychonauts also offer prayers for peace, protection and power.

The first ritualist says; "All is good here, all are well and strong. We are explorers, evolving, mutating and changing. We are psychonauts, we dare to develop and to grow".

One person has chosen to go through the initiation rite. That participant recalls:

Imagine being cocooned. Wrapped up tightly while naked in black coloured cling film or Saran wrap.

It begins at the ankles. Legs are bound together. Arms at the sides, each in turn captured and pinned down. The ripping sound of the film as sections are wound round the body, the person doing the mummification occasionally twisting the roll to create points of greater tension.

The wrapping is like a death shroud. The plastic is tight, though the person wrapping you takes care to ensure that you can breathe (the face is initially exposed, the tightness of the wrap is reduced around the neck). Finally the plastic covers the whole body with the exception of the head. That is when they ask you:

"Do you wish to make the journey?" to which I answer "Yes".

A mirror is held up beneath my head. A short tube is inserted gently up my left nostril. On the mirror are several lines of ketamine, smaller doses for the other members of this strange gathering and one big one. For me.

I determinedly snort half the line. The tube is inserted in my right nostril and I inhale the rest. The curious relationship between this practice and ancient Egyptian mummification (where the brain of the deceased is removed through the nostrils) pops into my mind. Then the sound starts again. The unrolling of cling film as my face is covered, an air hole made at my nose. What seems like layer upon layer is added until I cannot see. Though my ears are covered I can hear my companions taking their smaller doses of ketamine.

Am I okay? I'm asked, replying; "yes".

Then I say, "I think I'm going to fall over".

I feel the strong arms of my companions around me, easing me down. My body is stiff, I am tilted and realise that I am being laid to rest on a futon. The falling seems to take an age. I feel that I am the Djed column of ancient Egypt and I am toppling…

I realise that I have left my body. I can hear a woman somewhere talking. This is a guided visualisation. I am lying on a stone, inside a sarcophagus. I am inside a cube that reminds me of an iron pyrite crystal, greenish gold. The cube itself is inside a pyramid of bluish light. There is a night sky above me. The kind of sky you only get in the desert. I am locked in, beneath the depths of the Muladhara chakra.

There is silence. Out of the darkness peep millions of stars. I am beneath a blanket of innumerable celestial lights or perhaps within a cave spangled with fireflies. The fabric of space glitters with all these jewels. I have forgotten that I've taken a drug. Forgotten that I'm taking part in a ritual. Forgotten my body and not even aware that I am wrapped up like a parcel. There is only the darkness and the twinkling lights. There is nothing before this, there is nothing, there is nothing but this. I have always been here. In the dark, in this space, nothing is before…

Then there is a desire to move. I begin to hear speech outside of my world (though with no conception that there is an 'outside'). Something about moving from earth to water, something about birth.

There it is again—that desire to move.

And yet I do not move, I have no idea that I can move. I have forgotten my body, my limbs, and my form.

Then I can feel something, it starts at my feet as the words from outside get louder.

"...Ready to be re-born, to move and come into the light. From out of the earth into the waters of life..." There is music now, the rich tones of singing bowls, chanting and mantras. I feel my own chest resonate. I am intoning the mantra as well, a long, low Ommmmm, ahhhhhh, uhhhhhhh....

There it is at my ankles. Something is happening. A sound like cutting, the slitting of fabric.

It seems so fast. The feeling progresses up my body. In an instant it reaches my groin. There is a moment of fear. A cold sensation on my skin. Is it water, is it fluid? Am I being born? Do I have a body or am I emerging from my cocoon as nothing more than a flood of liquid?

Then I feel my legs. The ripping sensation moves up. I realise that the cold is from the bandage cutting scissors which are being used to open my wrapping.

As the volume of the voices grows I find myself joining in with the Bija mantra that is being sung, and moving. I can feel it now! I know that I have a definite form, a body of flesh and sinew and bone and lymph! I have four limbs and a rib cage! The binding is removed from my head. I have a head! A face, eyes, and I open them and smile.

They help me to sit and I look around. I have entered a space where we are each enlightened beings. We have crossed a spiritual abyss and now we sit together. Hands touching, our minds a communion of rapture. Each one of us a vast titan, like three giant statues of the Buddha. We sing blessing over a vessel of water. Into the ketamine space tumble words: "water, flow, keep it safe, keep it sacred, we are the water, share water, grok..."

The others have taken more ketamine and we are all at the same level now. We hold in our hands a vessel of water and can feel it pulsing with energy. Like a Ouija board planchette, it appears to move of its own accord. Great concentration (and yet a profound relaxation) is necessary to ensure that we don't drop this precious fluid ("Keep it safe, keep it sacred"). The movement of the vessel settles into a gentle circular motion and we breathe in unison.

"We are stirring the cauldron....
Turning the mill....
Water is the milk of the moon.
Share water...
(Keep it safe, keep it sacred...)
That all people might have water...
Clean and fresh...
The water of life..."

All these words, spoken by each person, weaving in and out, create a cycling invocation.

The circling stops, the water is held by just one participant, and they drink.

My companion offers me this water, mouth to mouth, in a kiss.

"May you never thirst."

I drink and the water slips inside me (I have an inside!). I take a sip and, also with a kiss, pass the magical fluid to the next person.

"May you never thirst".

The water passes round the circle, then we place it on a table, the soundtrack of mantra we've been using fades out.

We laugh, relax, and eventually, sleep.

The Medicine Circle

The term Medicine Circle may be used to describe any ceremony where the participants sit together, often through the night, and take sacred substances. In my experience of such things, a Medicine Ceremony begins around dusk and consists of various 'rounds' of activity. There are innumerable methods for holding a Medicine Ceremony and even within 'native' or 'traditional' contexts the ritual will have many variations (depending on the location, the style and skills of the person running the session etc.) and can be seen to change over time. Simply put, in terms of the ritual structure (as opposed to the spirit of the ceremony) there is no one 'right' or 'authentic' way to run a medicine circle.

The outline of a Medicine Ceremony given here is inspired predominantly by the design of the Native American peyote circle. The various elements described can be adapted, included or not depending on the size, style and belief systems of the people taking part.

Smaller groups of trippers, especially if they have experience of psychedelics and know each other well can create entheogenic ceremony with consensus decision making and collaboration. More complex roles and hierarchal approaches may suit ceremonial spaces with larger numbers of people and more novice psychonauts present.

A leading facilitator (the shaman, 'Medicine Carrier' or 'Roadman' in some traditions) has overall responsibility for the ritual. The leader's job is to 'hold the space' and determine the order of the ceremony. The leader of the ceremony should be trusted by participants and have a familiarity with the substances used. They need to display a calm, reassuring and authoritative attitude, providing a sanctuary within which people can meet with the medicines for themselves. (In peer-led groups a rotating leadership, perhaps through particular phases of the ritual, or other types of collaborative approaches may mean that there is no single leadership role.)

A leader may have several helpers.

Someone might have the role of perfuming the ritual site with suitable herbs. This acts as a punctuation mark in the ceremony, often to cleanse the space after a difficulty is encountered (e.g. a participant begins to cry as they touch on powerful emotions during prayer). This may be done by placing cedar, copal, pine, sage or other cleaning herbs on burning charcoal in a bowl or directly onto the hot embers of a central fire. A fan (often made from bird feathers) may be used to waft the smoke towards the person who needs it, and to drive the 'energy' of the 'heavy' prayer upwards toward the heavens.

Other purifying and reviving practices such as sage smudging, burning incenses or the use of perfumes such as Aqua de Florida (which is rubbed over the hands and forehead, and the invigorating floral scent inhaled) may form a round of activity or simply be used as and when the time feels right.

Depending on the tradition of the group, men and women may be segregated in the space (as they are in some Santo Daime Church meetings), with lines of men and women facing each other (and an altar and musicians/ritual leaders in the centre between the two groups). In other styles of working the whole group sits in a circle (limitations of space and larger group sizes may mean this becomes several concentric circles, though one large circle is usually seen as the best configuration).

There may be someone to guard and if necessary open the doorway to the space, someone to tend the central fire, and someone to play the drum. Other people may take up helper roles, especially where there are a large number of participants, perhaps to assist with people who are 'getting well' i.e. vomiting.

In some traditions, notably some of those that use of peyote and ayahuasca, the purgative effect of these medicines is imagined as part of the transformational process; hence the use of the expression 'getting well' (or even 'praying') rather than 'being sick'.

Whilst much is made of this aspect of Medicine Ceremony, it is rarely a major feature. Amongst a few dozen people there may be a small number who feel nausea at any point during their journeying. Therefore, it is simply sensible to have receptacles to hand. Small buckets and tissues are provided in the space for this purpose. Helpers may also be charged with assisting anyone who seems to be having other difficulties during the ceremony, and to ensure the general comfort (for example by providing blankets for warmth) and well-being of members of the group (these roles are particularly helpful when there are novice psychonauts and/or novice ritualists present).

Used tissues are generally burnt in a fire (though not usually the central fire) at the end of the ritual (prayers may be said at this point). Buckets may be washed out with water and their contents disposed of into a 'getting well hole'. This is a small hole dug into the earth (the turfs having being lifted off first). Any remaining flowers from the ritual could be placed on top of the relocated turfs when the hole is filled in at the end of the ceremony.

Where possible, participants are encouraged to be responsible for dealing with their own waste.

Depending on the style of the ritual members of the group may offer shamanic-style healing of the psychic energy body to others during the ceremony. No matter how these processes are imagined (whether as a placebo-like psychological trick, or as spirit intervention—or both) they are undoubtedly effective. If such healing is offered, and is appropriate to the ritual context, the recipient should clearly express their agreement. Given the emotionally charged interpersonal nature of the Medicine Circle, the whole group (and especially the key facilitators), should take care that a culture of mutual trust, respect and consent is maintained.

Personal Preparation

Every individual, whatever their role within the Medicine Circle (as facilitator or participant), should be comfortable that they are doing the right thing with the right people. Any animosity or other difficulty between members of the circle should be resolved before the ritual commences.

Many practitioners recommend particular diets before taking a sacred medicine (and sometimes afterwards too). A minimum half-day fast (taking only water and little else after a light midday meal, if the circle is in the evening) is very helpful, both to increase the effect of the medicine, and to make breakfast even more welcome (see below). Restraint from sexual activity is another process commonly used to focus attention on, and to increase anticipation of, the ceremony. Some practitioners like to refrain from sex for some time before, and sometimes also after the ceremony. These practices may be derived from a particular style or tradition of entheogenics or may emerge as insights from one's own practice. Other psychonauts may choose to not employ any of these constraints.

All participants should be mindful of the possible interactions between any medications and the drugs on offer. It is also generally helpful at the beginning of the ceremony to identify who in the group has not previously taken any of the medicine(s) being used. While novel physiological reactions to substances such as psychedelic cacti are extremely rare, they are not unknown.

Setting up the Space

A key element of the ritual is the central altar. Ideally everyone needs to be able to clearly see the altar, which acts as a visual focus throughout the rite. The altar will include items specific to the traditions of the participants; offerings suitable for the season, representations of the elements, natural objects such as flowers, images of spiritual teachers and cultural heroes etc. This altar is generally less of a workbench (ritual paraphernalia such as feather fans, smudge sticks of sage, musical instruments etc. are usually kept beside participants); instead it acts like a mandala. It is the visual focus for contemplation during the ritual.

The Medicine Circle includes a central fire of some sort. Candles may be used if the central space is a table size altar, and these are kept lit and replenished throughout the session. Alternatively, the fire may be something closer to the elaborate 'arrow-fire' of the traditional peyote circle (from which the glowing coals are swept out into the forms of birds or other shapes during the rite). The fire serves not only the practical function of providing light and warmth but is also the physical representation of the fire of the sun, the core of the earth, and the ever-transforming life-force (the 'Great Spirit' or 'Great Mystery').

The Fire Keeper ensures that the central fire is fed correctly and safely whatever its form (candles, charcoal or wood). The Fire Keeper is critical to the ceremony. This role is, in many respects, the most vital one for the Medicine Circle to be a success. One might make an analogy and say that the ritual leader or shaman is the driver of a steam train (the train being the ceremony, in which participants are the passengers). Staying with this metaphor, the Fire Keeper is the person who keeps the engine going.

In some rites a large bowl of water may be employed as the main focus; other groups may choose to use crystals or other objects. The qualities of reflectivity and light (which are enhanced by psychedelics) ensure that the altar successfully keeps the attention of participants. Whatever its form, the altar should be a thing of beauty and power (be that a witchy dark chthonic power or Zen-like simplicity). Collaborative creation of the central altar beforehand is a valuable element of ritual preparation.

Participants are generally encouraged to stay present in the ceremony by sitting up. Depending on the tradition this may be on chairs, but more often cross-legged or kneeling on the floor. For long periods of sitting on the ground, backrest chairs, animal skins, zafu meditation pillows and blankets can all be helpful. Participants need to be dressed in suitably warm, comfortable clothes. Depending on the style of the circle, 'native' costumes, plain white clothes, black robes or other garb may be appropriate. During the hours of sitting practice, participants may wish to stand, stretch or otherwise move. Rarely is the 'sitting' in a Medicine Circle completely static in the way that Zazen meditation is. While lying down may be acceptable within the group many people find that a relaxed seated posture and straight spine helps maintain the attention necessary to get the best out of the Medicine Ceremony. (However if the medicine is very strong it may be necessary to lie down whatever the 'expected' ritual behaviour.)

In a larger group setting it is common to select people who are 'strong in the medicine' (i.e. experienced with the drugs being used, especially in a ritual context) to sit at the cardinal points in the circle. These people serve as exemplars of how to sit throughout the rite and help hold the configuration of the ritual space.

Activities in a Medicine Circle may include:

Initial Prayers and Group Statement of Intent

At the beginning of the ritual prayers are made for a good, powerful, healing journey. If there is a specific intention for the Medicine Circle it may be spoken of here.

Depending on the style of the group, imaginal entities—ancestors, elemental powers of the directions, spirits of place, divine beings and other forces—may be called upon to bless, protect and empower the rite.

Participants may wish to hold hands and take some breaths together. (In Druidry three breaths are taken, one for the sky, one for the earth and one for the water. Sometimes a fourth breath is added, 'for the fire within our hearts'.)

Confession and Checking In

This process, if present, generally forms part of the opening of the ceremony. Participants may wish to state the problems they have, either as individuals, as a community, or on behalf of humanity as a whole. This part of the Medicine Circle allows people to express sadness at the difficulties and failures in life, acknowledging that which needs to be witnessed, with the tacit hope that the ceremony will assist in the transformation of these things.

These confessions can be spoken by participants in a whisper (while addressing the central fire) and/or simultaneously so that members of the group articulate their woes without becoming self-conscious.

Participants, perhaps passing a talking stick or other object round the circle, may want time to 'check in'. Each person expresses (in more or less detail depending on the intimacy of the group) what is going on in their life. They may talk about what feelings or questions they are coming to the ritual with and about any personal intention for the ceremony.

Taking the Medicine

In groups of more experienced psychonauts medicine may be available as and when participants wish. In more formal settings the shaman is the person primarily responsible for when rounds of medicine are provided, which substances are chosen and at what doses.

If a participant does not wish to take any medicine in either the first (or subsequent) rounds they may opt to simply bless themselves by placing their hands over the medicine and imagining its power entering them (this might be signified by a gesture such as raising the hands to the mouth, third eye etc. in order to imaginatively transfer the power into their bodymind).

The timing and amounts of booster doses during the ceremony is one of the key considerations for the group leader(s). The combination of medicines used also needs to be judged by the shaman. As well as being attentive to how people seem to be doing, it may be useful for the facilitator to periodically inquire how everyone is feeling (in terms of the psychedelic experience). A scale such as the Shulgin Scale, or another subjective calibration (e.g., between 1 = low and 5 = very high) could be used to establish how the medicine is working for participants.

A good medicine ceremony will serve to hold the psychedelic effect, enhance it and provide for the opportunity to experience this in a social context. Participants may of course ask for more medicine but should remember that baseline is relative and it is wise to give the sacrament a good amount of time to start working before asking for more. They also need to consider that larger doses may lead to a more internal process, while moderate doses may mean they can enjoy being a more active participant in the ritual.

Singing and Music

Musicians often provide a soundtrack to the ceremony, and songbooks can be used so everyone can join in with unfamiliar songs. In some Medicine Circles a drum is played (in Native American peyote rites this may be a water drum). The drum might be passed round the members of the circle or a designated drummer may come to sit beside the person singing to drum for them. A rattle and a staff to lean upon (if sitting) may be provided for the singer.

Songs may be anything from crowd-pleasing numbers where everyone can join in (e.g. Neo-Pagan chants or well-known medicine songs), to rune singing (galdr), Hindu Mantras, spontaneously arising made-up songs, glossolalia, vowel sounds, or songs from popular culture.

Those who do not wish to sing need not do so, but all are encouraged to take part, joining their voice to that of the group, if they can. Singing is not about being a great vocalist or performer but about helping to share and create the environment necessary for the collective journey. It is also a form of prayer. As with any music used during entheogenic experiments one benefit, particularly of rhythm, is that it provides a focus for attention and a sense of progression. This can help prevent participants getting stuck in mental loops, particularly those involving difficult emotions such a guilt, fear, shame etc. Singing provides a chance for people to experience joy, laughter, to be deeply moved, to transform trauma and sadness, to offer blessing and much more.

Members of the group may sing specific songs, instrumental or pre-recorded music may also form part of the ritual. The emotional qualities and lyrical content medicine songs are typically upbeat, positive, soulful, affirming and joyous. Songs that mention death, suffering etc. need not be excluded though the transformative potential of these challenges is typically emphasised. Some entheogenic traditions, especially those influenced by Catholic Christian syncretism, feature numerous songs that emphasis ideas such as the 'Divine Father' or 'Holy Mother' etc. For some people the content of these tunes may be distressing (for instance if they have suffered at the hands of an unkind parent). In more intimate groups (or if one is working as the shaman leading psychonauts from a particular group) the fact that song lyrics may trigger unwanted associations should be considered in advance. Look for songs with symbolism, metaphors and language that will resonate harmoniously with the group.

After songs have been sung some groups like to allow a short period of silence to let the atmosphere of the song 'sink in'. In other settings groups joyful cries of 'aho!' or clapping may follow a song.

Time for Silence and Stillness

At various points within the ritual it may be appropriate to have a period of silent, meditative reflection. This can be particularly potent if used for a time after the first dose of medicine is taken. Depending on the medicine used, a period of activity might be dedicated to inner-world journeying or collective dreaming. A single drum, singing bowl or pre-recorded audio could be used for these rounds.

Breaks

In some styles of ceremony, the aim may be to sit together as a group throughout the night. If so, a break may be offered around the middle of the night to allow people to get up, use the toilet, stretch their legs, go outside (if the ceremony is in a building) or to leave the circle for a while and relax. If the rite is inside, an outdoor fire could be prepared for members of the group to sit around to allow a little informal interaction to take place. The facilitator's role is to regulate the duration of any breaks and to ensure that all participants return to the ceremonial space for the next phase of the work, rather than wandering off into the darkness...

Taking Water

Drinking water may be provided during the middle of the night. This is done with due ceremony which helps to increase the appreciation of the refreshing draught and our reverence for its life giving properties. Water in the morning with breakfast, after a night with little to drink, is itself a potent Medicine. In other circles participants may keep their own supply of water to hand.

Prayers

Within the peyote circle model there are periods of prayer. These are most often made with tobacco that is smoked as the prayer is spoken. The effect of the tobacco is to re-centre the participant and to help them speak what is in their heart. A Medicine Circle rite may begin with each person smoking half of a tobacco cigarette (sometimes hand rolled using a corn husk in place of cigarette paper) while making prayers for a successful and powerful ceremony, and then laying the unsmoked half of the tobacco on the altar to represent their intention to stay with the ritual until the end. One of the final processes, at the end of a Medicine Circle that uses tobacco in this way, is that the remaining stubs of all the cigars used during the night are removed from the altar and burnt, along with cedar, in the central fire.

Often those smoking and praying will begin by blowing smoke upwards to the heavens, downwards to the earth, around them, and finally towards the central fire. A brief pause at this point is helpful to allow the tobacco to take effect. Prayers to the 'Great Spirit', 'Great Mystery' or some other name suited to the style of the circle are then uttered. These prayers are frequently those of gratitude, but may include any heart-felt outpourings the speaker feels inspired to say, including words about difficulties they are experiencing in their lives. Prayers can also be made silently. Generally, the person praying addresses their prayer to the central altar/fire.

Prayerful activity or other periods of talk could also be signalled by passing round an object such as a talking stick instead of tobacco.

Movement

There may be a period of time during which the facilitator feels that it would be helpful for the group to move, to stretch and perhaps dance. This may include the use of live or pre-recorded music (as selected by the shaman and/or group in advance of the session). Dancers should ensure that they do not distract those who remain seated and looking at the central fire. People managing the space may request that dancers step outside the main (seated) circle, or occupy a particular part of the ritual chamber. Rituals that are predominantly focused on dancing will have the reverse rule; where people who want to sit and rest will be asked to retire behind the position of dancing participants.

Other Activities

Other rounds of activity within the circle could include storytelling, guided imagery journeys, drawing, breathwork, indeed any activity that suits the medicines used and the style of the group. Readings from inspiring texts, reciting poetry, even beatboxing or charades may be appropriate. Be creative and build a Medicine Circle design that suits you and your community.

Ceremonial Behaviour

Depending on the style of the Medicine Circle there may be various conventions about how one behaves in the space. Examples of customary practices that the group may use include:

Objects (e.g. tobacco smokes or the bowl containing the medicine) are passed first towards the fire and then handed on to the next person. Thus these objects symbolically (and depending on the receiver's state of consciousness possibly literally) appear from out of the fire.

Tobacco smokes are held between the finger and thumb, orientated so that the burning tip faces the person holding it and the other end points towards the central fire.

When moving in the space, care is taken not to pass between the fire and anyone who is praying, singing, drumming, 'getting well' or taking medicine (the medicine is usually placed in front of the group leader when not being consumed). The only person who does not need to abide by this role is the individual charged with tending the central fire.

In general all movements in the space should feel 'harmonious'. This may mean that participants are encouraged to move clockwise (in the direction of the sun in the northern hemisphere) or in other ways that are deemed appropriate. The aim here is to bring attention to how the space is constructed 'energetically' (which could be interpreted as a way of imagining the interpersonal relations within the group as a type of social geometry). Skilful leader(s) will be aware of how people are moving in the space, with what level of attention, and will in some (usually fairly subtle way) intervene, kindly, to correct any kinks or breaks in the flow of the ceremony cause by a 'mistake', smoothing out the interpersonal energy (relationships) within the room.

People who are experiencing powerful or difficult trips may have a blanket offered to them by a helper but within many medicine circles it is generally considered best to allow people to get on with their own inner work. Unless there is significant distress or a need expressed for assistance a person who is, for example, weeping would be left to their own process. As mentioned above, there may be exceptions to this policy within some groups (especially ones where participants know each other well), where one or more people may offer shamanic-style 'energetic' healing.

When participants are speaking (for example when praying) it is often helpful to have a word or phrase that marks the end of their speech. This prevents anyone accidentally interrupting when the person talking is simply pausing for thought. In North American style Medicine Circles the word 'Aho' is often used. This is a shortened form of 'Aho Mitakuye Oyasin', which roughly translated means 'these words' (e.g. prayer, song etc.), 'are for all my relations' (i.e. all beings). The word Aho or 'Ho' may also be used as an agreement (the equivalent of the British parliamentary 'hear, hear!' or the Christian 'amen!') in response to what is being said. Some modern European Medicine Circles instead use the word 'ahoy!' with the nautical implication of 'I see (i.e. bear witness to) it'.

Talk is minimised when sitting together in the Medicine Circle so that idle conversations do not disrupt the whole group or individual processes. Practitioners are encouraged to keep their eyes on the central fire rather than looking round the room or at other people during the session. An exception to this, within a larger ritual setting, is found in the role of the person providing the ritual cleaning smoke (in the peyote circle 'Cedar Woman'). As she lays down the incense and wafts this with a fan she is might look across the fire at the person receiving the smoke and gently smile.

Breakfast

Around dawn food is ritually prepared for the group. In the peyote circle this is traditionally done by four women who are asked to bring in a breakfast of fruit, corn, deer meat and water. Songs and prayer are used to consecrate the food and final ritual processes (e.g. burning the last tobaccos) take place before the meal is eaten. In this way participants can enjoy that last bit of stoic patience (if they are engaging with the determined 'warrior style' of sitting) that has kept them going through the night, and finally break their fast and leave the circle.

Approach of the Ritual

The aim of the Medicine Circle ceremony is to create a space for individuals to work through their own private process in a setting that is powerful and supportive. Especially when the phenylethylamine family of sacraments are used (e.g. peyote, San Pedro, Sassafras etc.), the general atmosphere of the session is one of gratitude, heart-chakra opening, community, shared humanity, trust and joy. The usual aim is to use the positive healing vibe of the ceremony to push sadness and trauma out of the psyche of each participant with a wave of concentrated, entheogenically enhanced, acceptance, fellowship and happiness.

Adaptation of the Medicine Circle

No two medicine circles are the same. Whether a crescent altar is used (typical in the Native American Church) or Christian liturgical prayers (common in the syncretic ayahuasca using traditions), is a matter for individual experience, taste and the collective identity of the group. Medicine circles can be peer-led groups or settings in which one or more experienced psychonauts act as shaman to hold space for those who are new to the process.

Aftercare

After the ritual meal a chance to share further food, time to chill out, relax and rest is important. It is obviously essential to return to a good baseline level of awareness before driving. Opportunity for a nap before leaving the ceremonial site might prove welcome.

Spirituality and Fun

While the Medicine Circle as presented in this context is framed as an entheogenic spiritual process, it is also something people enjoy (even if a given trip features challenging content). This challenges the assumptions of there being a distinction between spirituality (which, in Protestant Christian terms, means denial and suffering) and recreation (which is sometimes looked at as unfavourably sensualist and Fallen in some belief systems). In the diversity of shamanic and tribal settings in which psychoactive drugs are taken some cultures emphasise the spiritual aspects of the process, others the social and recreational. In one sense the night long vigil, led by the shaman, is the prototype of the Western rock music festival or rave; a series of rounds (of different music, art and other entertainments) plus some intoxicating substances thrown in to make it all more interesting. While this type of collective group ritual may be approached with a spiritual intention to the fore, consideration should also be given to the playful and even trickster like aspects of the set, setting and substances of this approach.

Where to Find Your Circle

It can be very helpful to find an established Medicine Circle to take part in, whether this is in an exotic far-flung location or part of an underground movement, before trying your hand at creating one for yourself. That said if you don't have access to those communities or people with those skills an intelligent group of friends, equipped with the information here (plus a little more research and creative flair), could easily create their own ritual.

Although a peyote medicine circle often involves participants staying together all night, if the psychedelic used is of a shorter duration the time spent in the circle may be reduced as with this example:

Dawn of the Toad

Looking out from the Temple the bright sun of May Day begins to rise. There are five of us, a pipe and the medicine, 5-MeO-DMT, the venom of the Sonoran Desert Toad. We are in a safe and fabulously beautiful space, we ask that people in the circle don't chat; we want to stay focused on the ceremony.

The pipe is loaded. One person holds a drum, this they irregularly tap, stroke, and softly coax into gentle rhythmic patterns. Another person sings, their voice a funny and beautiful extemporary sound ranging from Siberian style throat singing, the imitated drone of the didgeridoo, to Asian mantra-like humming.

I inhale. The sun streaming into the temple glints on the marble floor. I kneel down on the reindeer skin we're going to take turns sitting on as we make our journeys (nothing like flying on a magical reindeer through the psychedelic skies!). The intensity of the trip rises up; I am falling down into the earth. The drumbeats and song see me through and, as I begin to come back to myself, I open my mouth and join the song. Soft voices from the others in the circle weave in and out, echoing in the chamber and singing in the psychedelic dawn.

I place my hands together over my heart, wordlessly give thanks and smile.

The pipe is loaded again and I pass it and my place on the animal fur to the next traveller. This time I take up the song, letting my mouth find the sounds as the drum tap, tap, taps and the shaman beside me inhales.

Once we have all journeyed we all hold hands together for a moment, breathe together. We informally say words to thank the medicine for being with us this morning; we smile, hug each other and drift off to forage for breakfast...

The basic format of sitting together in a medicine circle can be greatly adapted depending on the nature of the group and the substance employed, as with the following example of a ritual with *Salvia divinorum*.

Divine Silence

We have decided to explore the Salvia spirit. Two of us have some experience with this power plant; two are completely new to it. We know the Salvia journey works best in silence and darkness so we have got four sleeping spaces ready in the living room. There are blankets and cushions and just a few low lights as we begin.

We are using dried leaves and we've checked the dosage information using erowid.org. We've determined that two grams of the herb is approximately one heaped teaspoon full. Our two novices with this medicine opt to take a low dose (two grams) and the more experienced shamans opt for a 'common' dose (six grams).

Before we begin, we clean our teeth, brushing the gums and insides of our cheeks to maximise the absorption of the medicine which we will mix in individual bowls with a little warm water and chew for about 20 minutes. The bowls of medicine are prepared as we sit in a circle. In the centre of the circle we bring a live salvia plant. We introduce ourselves to the plant and ask for its blessing and wisdom: "Salvia spirit we are pleased to meet you, thanks for coming all this way from the Mazatec people of Mexico. We honour you this night and hope that you can take us on a wonderful journey, showing us your power in a good way. Ahoy!" Each person speaks to the plant, addressing it like a valued friend, a guest, a teacher, words are heartfelt but informal.

One of the four in the circle takes the bag of salvia leaves. "I've been collecting these for two years", he says, "I hope that we can honour this medicine which is new to many of us here, and learn from each other". (As well as the idea that the spirit of the plant is a teacher there is also the notion that the plant spirit learns from the experience of interfacing with human culture and neurology.)

Then the chewing begins.

A very low ambient music track, timed to last for twenty minutes plays and as it ends we can feel the medicine coming on. The already low lighting is extinguished.

Each person lays down, goes silent, and we enter the salvia space.

Any sound is distracting, even annoying and I reflect that next time ear plugs might help. The journey lasts about an hour and as each of us feels that we have come out of the trance we leave the room (as agreed beforehand) and quietly make our way to another part of the house to drink tea together before retiring, maintaining low lighting, soft voices and gentleness, ready to continue the ritual in our dreams.

In the morning we all gather to thank the salvia plant and the remains of unswallowed chewed leaves are taken outside and returned to the earth.

A Guide for the Perplexed

One way of exploring psychedelics is to do so in the company of someone who facilitates the experience for the psychonaut. This approach is favoured in Western psychotherapeutic contexts. A therapist or guide is on hand to help the psychonaut focus on a healing objective that is decided before the session. This method is a powerful breakthrough therapeutic tool for issues such as addictions, post-traumatic stress disorder and other mental and psychosomatic illnesses. Guide or therapist is a specialist role that implies an excellent understanding of the medicine being used (including personal experience of its effects) and the psychotherapeutic process. (In psychedelic therapy drug enhanced sessions are usually part of a longer process that includes non-psychedelic sessions.)

A sitter is a person who performs the role of caring for or accompanying the psychedelicized subject but who is not necessarily there in a therapeutic capacity. A sitter can provide greater safety for the psychonaut when they are using a new substance, taking a high dose, or perhaps exploring a material where they may behave in ways that are dangerous (for example when using deliriants such as datura, or substances where they may try to get up and move around while intoxicated and come to harm, such as smoked *Salvia divinorum*). They can also subsequently provide a source of narrative verification, amusing anecdotes, or integration, in addition to acting as a valued companion on an adventure.

Unlike the shaman, the sitter or guide usually doesn't take the drug the psychonaut consumes. Occasionally the guide may take a threshold or micro level dose (to be 'on the same wavelength'). Ideally a sitter should have familiarity with the particular drug the psychonaut is using and should have personal experience of the psychedelic state.

The sitter's role is to help create and maintain a safe, pleasant setting for the psychonaut. They should read up on the substance the psychonaut has chosen to use so that they feel confident that they can deal with any psychological or physiological problems that may arise, and steer attention towards the positive aspects of the experience if necessary. This may mean being aware that the drug used may provoke nausea, or that it should not be combined with certain medications or foods, and ensuring suitable props (cushions, art materials etc.) are to hand.

Before the session the sitter should assess the set and setting for the trip. They should familiarise themselves with the space(s) in which the journey will take place, and feel confident that they can fulfil their role to support the psychonaut. Choices of music and other stimulus for the session should be discussed before the experiment.

During the session the sitter ensures the comfort of the psychonaut; offering water, blankets, changes of music or lighting as directed by the psychonaut. Given the sensitive nature of the psychedelic state it's good to remember that 'less is more'; if the psychonaut encounters difficulties in their trip changing the music, allowing fresh air into the room, or offering a blanket to snuggle with is often all that is needed.

The sitter should strive to remain non-judgmental about the content that emerges during the trip. Sitters may want to provide gentle, non-sexual physical contact to reassure the psychonaut by holding their hand or touching their upper arm. The sitter provides a constant, background, reassuring presence with their relaxed body posture and kindly smile. Talk may be kept to a minimum, with the sitter repeating back to the psychonaut any positive phrases that emerge in the journey, providing encouragement that all is well.

The sitter should stay with the psychonaut until both parties are happy that the psychonaut has reached baseline consciousness. They may wish to make themselves available for follow-up discussions with the psychonaut a day or two after the trip.

Dealing with Challenges

Depending on the context in which difficult experiences occur, and the substance(s) in question there are many ways of dealing with the challenges that can arise in the psychedelic experience. You may find yourself needing to support another person or you may find yourself needing to change how your own trip is unfolding. The three variables of set, setting and substance are the means by which difficulties such as anxiety, emotional downward spirals etc. can be addressed and the trajectory of the trip changed.

Remember that the 'work' of the psychedelic journey can involve facing our fears and other difficult psychological content. These processes can be vital part of the transformative power of the trip and are not necessarily to be avoided.

Changing the Setting

Turning the volume of music down (or up), changing the mood of the sounds, altering the lights, or offering comforting blankets and cushions are simple ways in which the setting of trip can be changed.

If the environment itself is not safe or has some other major problem for the psychonaut, it is best to go somewhere else. If a person is available to assist in gently moving the tripper from one environment to another that can be a great help.

Often indoor environments provoke introspection. Just going outside to a safe (and ideally beautiful) space can be a powerful way to change the direction of trip from something that feels 'too inward' to one with a more expansive positive feel.

Changing the Set

Breathing slowly and easily will often have a marked effect on the mental state of someone in psychedelic distress. Another method is to find a particularly delightful or empowering memory and review that. Changing the focus of attention, 'just listen to the music' is often all that is needed because the psychedelic consciousness is so plastic (i.e. able to be manipulated; by the psychonaut themselves, as well as external influences).

If you are alone try to change your own perceptions. For instance, if you meet scary psychedelic snakes try reimaging the movements you perceive as those of something less threatening (e.g. growing plants).

Rather than repressing or ignoring challenging mental content explore it, change your relationship with it and find the best way to sit with and transform these feelings. You may like to try dialoguing with difficulties, aloud or silently as appropriate.

It may be useful to make a metaphorical link between external stimulus and inner transformation; an example of this could be to imagine that with each beat of the music the 'knot' of tension that is the core of some psychic distress is becoming unwound. Identifying and using these kinds of metaphorical relationships is the basis of mimetic magic (described above) and, in the depths of the psychedelic state, is a very powerful technique for personal transformation.

Adopting an open bodily posture, or sitting up in a relaxed yet alert way (as one might when meditating) are simple ways to change the set. Playing with facial expressions (e.g. smiling) can provoke instant, powerful results.

Changing the Substance

Where there is clear evidence of a bad reaction to a drug (breathing or pulse issues, or other definite physiological problems—do make sure that anyone checking these signs is in a fit state themselves to judge competently!) it is wise to seek medical attention. If there is someone around who has not taken the medicine get their support and advice before summoning medical help.

Pay attention to clear physiological signs of distress. If you feel faint sit down! If the psychonaut becomes unconscious check that they are in a safe place. Put them into the recovery position or otherwise check that their airway is clear (especially if they are vomiting or likely to do so). Periods of unconsciousness, characterized by reduced muscle tone and immobility or by seizures, can and do happen occasionally on psychedelic drugs (generally at higher dose, or when the psychonaut is in a sensitive state. Unconsciousness is of course to be expected with anesthetizing sacraments such as ketamine or nitrous oxide). In all cases check the pulse and breathing. Keep the practitioner safe (for example if they are having a fit and likely to flail around). Dissociative states caused by classic psychedelics will usually pass in less than 20 minutes and cause no lasting damage (subjectively the psychonaut may be having a wonderful innerworld adventure!) but these events can be distressing for those looking after the unconscious individual. It may therefore be beneficial to talk through what happened after the psychedelic session.

Physiological problems are remarkably rare with well-known psychedelics (which is why they are popular); these are very safe medicines. Even apparently organic problems with breathing or nausea are much more likely to be the result of anxiety and psychic distress rather than 'bad acid'.

If, as is likely, the psychonaut is simply 'freaking out' (and others present are competent to assess this) it would not be wise to call for an ambulance. Hospital environments are unlikely to provide the best setting for a psychedelic experience. At a festival there may be spaces specifically set up to support people who are experiencing challenging trips staffed by competent psychedelic sitters. If you use psychedelics at a festival it is worth memorising the location of such services, or ways of summoning assistance, well in advance of any potential need arising.

When assisting a psychonaut try to stay open and calm. The supporters act as exemplars of the relaxed and easy state of mind they wish to communicate to the person having a challenging journey.

There are various methods for checking how a person is doing psychologically. Asking simple questions; their name, address, and the date many prove useful. The supporter should be aware that the person experiencing the bad trip may well be paranoid and so care should be taken when speaking. In practice it is often more useful to find a phrase that seems to help; 'you are coming through this journey and transforming yourself' and stick with variations of that rather than engaging in more elaborate dialogue. Humour and even laughter can be beneficial but may also be misunderstood and so an accepting, calming approach is advised.

Smoking of various herbs may provide the opportunity for a 'prayerful' pause. Tobacco, used in this way, has the benefit of helping to re-centre the mind. Cannabis can also be used in order to help the tripper chill out.

There are few useful home remedies that will turn off (or turn down) the psychedelic experience. There is little point in taking vitamin C in order to stop being high although 'come down' placebo of some form may be useful, depending on the situation. (Shamanic healing can be thought of as the deployment of a range of strategies that invoke the placebo effect. When combined with the actual use of powerful mind altering drugs the placebo effect has even greater power than usual, including the ability to dramatically reduce or even turn-off the psychedelic experience.)

There is may be some benefit in using coca leaves in low dose to reduce the intensity of tryptamine trips, though it is worth considering that turning off a trip with these or other pharmacological interventions (such as tranquilisers or antipsychotic medications) can itself cause later psychological problems and a sense of 'unfinished business'.

Relax and Float Downstream

For the vast majority of difficult psychedelic journeys, the best course of action is to ride it out. Find a safe and supportive space, fill your mind with positive messages and things to engage your attention (e.g. music, the natural world etc.), slow the breath and relax.

The key to working with psychedelic drugs is to open up and let the medicine work through you, even when this feels difficult. It's important to remind oneself, and be reminded if necessary by others, that you will not die (yet), that you are on a drug and this experience will stop in time. Remember the psychedelic mantra for challenging trips; 'this too shall pass'.

Many of the techniques in this book can be used to address or modify major challenges in the psychedelic state. They can also be used as ways to change our attention and get us out of those less difficult but still tiresome mental loops that may accompany a trip (such as obsessively looking for a missing CD or repeatedly trying, and failing, to position candles successfully in candlesticks).

Refining Your Rapture

This slogan is a reminder that the use of mind altering substances can easily become a consumerist pursuit of the 'bigger and better buzz' unless our relationship with drugs is managed successfully. Increasing dosage, particularly when it comes to psychedelics, often leads to diminishing returns because of the psychological and physiological tolerances that can rapidly develop. In many cases a better, healthier, safer (and less expensive) way to explore these substances is to use techniques such as fasting, as well as the methods detailed in this book, to get higher with less.

Salvia divinorum provides an excellent example of how less can be more. If the leaves are chewed in silent darkness, and the user strives to be attentive to the spirit of the plant, all manner of amazing visions may appear. It is also possible to make a concentrated extract of the plant and to inhale large amounts of salvinorin rich smoke using a bong. The latter method is much stronger and faster but usually lacks the depth and unfolding beauty of the chewed salvia vision. Smoked salvia can be very disorientating and at high doses is likely to lead to amnesia of the experience itself. Simply put; more is not necessarily better.

The concept of the 'heroic' dose unfortunately disregards this axiom, and while for some materials there may be one or more 'breakthrough' points (where the state presented by the psychedelic undergoes a step change) this is not simply a function of dose.

The techniques described in this book are intended to increase our sensitivity to the psychedelic state (in part so we can notice and manifest the amazing insights from these experiences in our day-to-day lives). By holding the psychedelic state in a powerful, secure way (through intention, ritual and other practices) the experience becomes (potentially) safer *and* stronger. This means that while a shaman may be able to take 'heroic' amounts of drugs and still run the ceremony, they will often also be able to take a very small amount and still feel the hit.

Sometimes it is beneficial to have a full-on experience and push the envelope of our minds, sometimes it is better to explore a mid-range dose (especially if we are using ceremonial style practices or combining our psychedelics with activities such as walking or visiting museums) and sometimes microdosing and abstinence are useful. The intelligent psychonaut does not confuse quantity with quality.

On Coming Down

Psychedelic drugs, especially when we are deep in the trip, make us present in the Now (much like meditative practices). Often one notices that one is coming down the moment that a reflective narrative emerges within the trip, 'do you remember earlier in the night, when the mushrooms were really strong?...'

Many psychedelic drugs have very positive after-effects (the 'afterglow') although body load may occasionally produce an unpleasant 'hangover'. The wise shaman discovers how to positively integrate all after-effects, to mitigate any difficult symptoms, and allow the greatest possible benefit from the psychedelic voyage to emerge as the practitioner returns to their baseline state of awareness.

Time is the great integrator. After any major psychedelic adventure (especially one that lasts several hours, such as with LSD or MDMA) it is important to allow time to rest. Nourishment and good sleep are important to allow the experience of the trip to settle into the deepest parts of the bodymind.

Following a powerful trip you may want to eat some good solid food and spend a little time in a natural environment if one is available to you. Smudging with sage or perfuming the space with suitable incense can also be beneficial, as can opening the windows to let fresh air in. Clear away the debris of the party/ceremony, shower or bathe, and relish the experience of coming back to baseline. Being high is great but taking delight in the post-drug afterglow and 'respecting the Medicine' matters (that is, using the time to appreciate what has happened).

If you had challenges in the journey reflect on them, learn from them, and congratulate yourself on having passed through the ordeal.

Remember that even (or even especially!) positive, earth-shatteringly brilliant trips also take time to integrate and recover from. The astounding beauty of full-on psychedelic visuals/sensorial experiences are awe inspiring. 'Making sense' of what has transpired is not necessary in the immediate hours following the trip. Enjoy existing, take notes of the world shattering philosophies you have discovered, and be prepared to find them somewhat obscure the next week in retrospect... A healthy application of kindness to one's self and others goes a long way to building good relations over the years with this kind of activity.

It is generally wise to wait to take action on any insights that you felt you 'had to do' during your trip. Allow yourself to sleep, to dream, and some critical distance so that you can judge how to skilfully manifest your psychedelic vision in the world.

To encourage sleep low doses of gentle substances such as chamomile tea, cannabis or alcohol may be helpful. While some psychonauts like to use supplements (such as 5-HTP) after psychedelic adventures any hangover or depression following an experience, such as an all-night rave, is most likely due to tiredness rather than neurochemical deficit.

After you have come down from your trip be prepared to feel great! The afterglow of a well-managed psychedelic session will usually leave you feeling healthy, calm and alert. There can be a sense that your mind has been reset, that your attention has received a cosmic spring clean and that your body is relaxed and happy. Enjoy these sensations and try to build on them with each trip and while in your baseline awareness.

Be attentive in the days and weeks that follow and allow yourself time to mull over and appreciate what you have experienced. You may find memories of the psychedelic state surface in your waking hours. These may be triggered by a stimulus that you associate with the state (such as the repetitive beats of dance music) or you may dream about what has happened. Acknowledge these effects, appreciating the teaching of the medicine and how it has changed you.

It may be helpful to record a trip report and perhaps share this with others (there are several online archives of such reports, notably at erowid.org and psychonautwiki.org).

Make offerings of thanks to the spirits, your gods or to the wonder of your own neurochemistry.

Acknowledging the Three Blessings

After a powerful moment of ritual (with or without medicine) this ceremony can be used to express our gratitude.

Hold the hands in prayer position on the crown of the head. Bring attention to the lineage of teachers who have allowed you to get to this moment in your own spiritual development or personal quest for meaning.

Depending on your style you can imagine the sandals of your guru on your head, and their guru on top of them. A great line of teachers stretching into the sky. You might instead choose to imagine this as a community of stars above you. All those wise people, cunning folk, shamans, explorers and many others who, now, in the past and in the future, have been engaged with the philosophies and techniques of magic and sacred Medicine. There may be particular teachers, living or dead that you want to bring your attention to in this moment. This act recognises that we are part of the sangha (community) of these practitioners, in all their myriad forms and traditions.

Next, move the hands, still in prayer position, down so that the thumbs press on the third eye or Ajna chakra. With this movement bring attention to yourself. You may think of this as the unique and indivisible diamond Atman of your existence. Or you may imagine the self as being the confluence of many forces, acting in the past, present and future. You might wish to pay attention to yourself as a 'conspiracy of selves' or to recognise your own unique narrative (or a combination of all of these interpretations of the Self). In this moment we pay homage to us—our individuality and sense of identity.

Finally, the hands are held in prayer at the heart. Bring attention to those beings that support you. Those who love and care for you, who feed and nurture you. This could include humans and other creatures you love, what you eat, the air you breathe. The focus of attention here is on the sense of being loved, nourished and cared for. This is a moment for appreciating those aspects of the universe that provide you with a sense of being valued.

Having spent as long as you need to with this practice, go and do something else. Let your acknowledgement of these blessings be absorbed into the background reality of your daily life.

Ahoy!

Online Resources

theblogofbaphomet.com/getting-higher

Made in the USA
Middletown, DE
28 December 2019

81963904R00080